THE UN
HOLE

Unionist Activity and Local Conflict in Western Virginia

David Scott Turk

HERITAGE BOOKS
2008

HERITAGE BOOKS

AN IMPRINT OF HERITAGE BOOKS, INC.

Books, CDs, and more—Worldwide

For our listing of thousands of titles see our website
at
www.HeritageBooks.com

Published 2008 by
HERITAGE BOOKS, INC.
Publishing Division
100 Railroad Ave. #104
Westminster, Maryland 21157

Copyright © 1994 David Scott Turk

Other books by the author:

A Family's Path in America: The Lees and Their Continuing Legacy

Give My Kind Regards to the Ladies: The Life of Littleton Quinton Washington

*The Memorialists: An Antebellum History of Alleghany, Craig,
and Monroe Counties of Western Virginia, 1812-60*

International Standard Book Numbers
Paperbound: 978-0-7884-0029-2
Clothbound: 978-0-7884-7048-6

TABLE OF CONTENTS

Introduction......ix

Prologue......xiii

What the War Did......1

Chapter One--The Opening Year--1861......11

Chapter Two--Southern Pendulum--1862......27

Chapter Three--Horse and Saber--1863......47

Chapter Four--The Elephant has Arrived--1864......77

Chapter Five--Swords into Plowshares--1865......94

Afterward--Remembering......100

Appendix--108th Virginia Militia Rosters......107

Bibliography......116

Index......125

ABOUT THE AUTHOR

David Scott Turk is a graduate student at George Mason University and works in the field of history. He is a native Washingtonian and has family roots in western Virginia since the 1700's. He has written the <u>Bostic Family of Monroe County, West Virginia</u> (1988) and many articles on the history of western Virginia. He is married to the former Janet Vogel and lives in Fairfax, Virginia.

ACKNOWLEDGMENTS

This work would not have been possible without the help of some very fine people. My long-suffering wife Janet sanitized the footnotes and endured my long research trips. Dr. Elizabeth L. Hudgins gave my manuscript life. My neighbor Elaine White was able to make sense of it. Special mention is give to neighbor Marifae Hudgins and her dachshund, Heidi.

There are too many people to thank for their help while on my research endeavors. Stewart Bostic and his wife Marie opened their house and knowledge to us. Mr. Layman Reynolds' fascinating family knowledge was instrumental. Also, my sincere thanks to all those who helped put this together: correspondents, archivists, researchers, and family.

On the academic end, Drs. Gilbert Millar and Donald Crowl of Longwood College encouraged me in my earlier pursuits of history as a career. Also contributing to my style are Drs. Ken Bowling and Charlene Bickford of the First Federal Congress Project, and Frederick S. Calhoun.

Finally, I thank my parents, my late grandfather, and my late neighbor, C. Turner Hudgins. This book is dedicated to Mr. Hudgins for always showing the courage to stand up for something, even if it was unpopular. In a way, that's what this book is about. C. Turner Hudgins embodies his work.

D.S.T.
October 1993

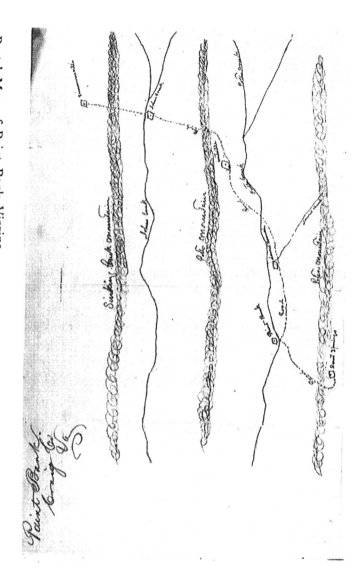

Postal Map of Point Bank, Virginia.
Courtesy of the National Archives.

INTRODUCTION

I saw the valley that would change my life for the first time in 1976. I was a twelve year old at the time, and my family was on vacation in the Carolinas. My Grandfather came with us on the trip, and we decided to search for the home of his childhood. Unfortunately, after we found it, the threat of snakes in the overgrown grasses and underbrush kept us from walking up to the family cemetery located on a nearby hill. Luckily, we weren't hampered from taking a long look at the house. What had once been a wooden frame house was now covered with a flagstone veneer. If my grandfather was disappointed at the condition of the house, or our unwillingness to traipse through the tall grass to the cemetery, he didn't show it.

Still, there was something memorable about that place for me. Perhaps the condition of the road caused me to feel something special: the car had to climb the twists and turns of Potts' Mountain, struggling like an early settler against the rough terrain and twisty dirt roads. Perhaps it was just knowing that my family came from there. At any rate, something lead me to the pursuit of my family history.

By the time I was twenty one, I had begun a serious study of genealogy. I constantly questioned my relatives, begging them to tell me stories of their youths. Eventually, this study led me to return to the Back Valley and to Grandfather's homeplace. Oddly, I still remembered all of the turns, even the final one up to the old house.

During this on-going search for my family history, I discovered the pension record pertaining to Morgan Taylor Jarvis, a brother of my great-great-grandmother, Jane Jarvis Bostic. As I read the record, I discovered that he had been a Union soldier, not a Confederate as I had originally thought! Further probing revealed that Jane's cousins enlisted in the Union Army. In addition, several of Jane's relatives had fled to Ohio to escape the Conscription Act of 1862. More of her relatives aided Confederate deserters and Federal troops. A major discovery, however, occurred after my grandfather's death in 1990. In my reading of Southern Claims Commission records, I found that his great-grandfather had been an active member of a secret Unionist society.

This was difficult for me to swallow. I had believed that my ancestors were uniformly Confederate in their views and actions. One relative was upset enough to ask, "We don't have to tell anyone, do we?" Still, I hope that in relating the story I will shed light on Unionist activities of some western Virginia families.

Even in the Unionist actions of many of the Southerners, one finds people deeply devoted to their region yet willing to go against their neighbors because of their beliefs. Though deeply committed Southerners, it may come as a surprise that a good deal of the population in western Virginia looked to the Union and President Abraham Lincoln. Some named their children after Lincoln.

Paint Bank, in Craig County, was the core of what local citizen George A. Linton called the "Union Hole."

However, the spread of Unionism reached far beyond Craig County. Three counties show a great deal of evidence for wide-spread Unionism with one family particularly involved. The Jarvis family represented families split apart by hunger, war, and varying sympathies. This study focuses on the Jarvis family due to the great amount of available information on it. Many other families from that region could have served as a substitute. Genealogy meets historical study for me at this point. I hope that the two merge peacefully for the reader, but, if the narrative appears choppy or inconsistent, I apologize for the personal liberties I have taken to explain the origins of the "Union Hole."

Field A. Jarvis about 1880. Courtesy of Lafe Armentrout.

PROLOGUE

THE JARVIS FAMILY IN WESTMORELAND COUNTY, VIRGINIA: PLANTERS IN TOBACCO SOCIETY

Like many families of the Colonial period, the Jarvis Family emigrated from the British Isles to seek a better life in America. The tobacco culture of the newly settled Eastern Shore of Virginia provided just that opportunity, but it also brought the risk of misfortune. Life was simple, short, and hard. Still, while there were many Jarvis immigrants, most came from England to the Eastern Shore of Virginia, and specifically to Accomack or Northampton County. Most of the other family members moved to the more populated Tidewater region of Virginia. [1]

The first Jarvis traced for the Monroe County, West Virginia, ancestry is Richard Jarvis. All indications point to the probability that Richard was, at one time, an indentured servant, though there is no direct reference to this in the Westmoreland County records.

---

[1] Susie M. Ames, ed., County Court Records of Accomack--Northampton, Virginia 1640-1645 Vol. 10 (Charlottesville: Press of Virginia, 1973), 8-9; Ibid., 46; Ibid., 209; Orville Bostic Interview, Fairfax, VA, June 1989; Clayton Torrence, comp., Virginia Wills and Administrations 1632-1800 (Richmond: William Byrd Press through National Society of Colonial Dames of America, 1930), 230.

Richard Jarvis first appeared in the Westmoreland records in July of 1684, when John Foxhall, a local mill owner sued Richard over the estate of Artmanus Wagamaster. In an order book dated January 19, 1691/92, Richard appeared again as the defendant in a court case settling the estate of Patrick Miskill. When Richard died, his estate was meager.[2]

The first mention of Richard's sons is also found in these old order books. "John Jarvis, son of Richard is by consent of his father bound apprentice to James Bourn. Ordered hee serve James Bourn in such imployment as hee shall have occasion untill hee be twenty years of age" (Nov. 30, 1693).[3]

A second Richard Jarvis was found in Westmoreland and Stafford County records. According to further documentation, his descendants remained in that area. A third Richard Jarvis was found in the 1778 records of Prince William County, Virginia.[4]

---

[2] John Frederick Dorman, Westmoreland County, Virginia, Order Books 1660-1698, Part III, 1682-1684 (Washington, D.C.: n.p., 1985), 65; Dorman, Westmoreland County, Virginia, Order Books 1660-1698, Part I, 1690/1-1692 (Washington, D.C.: n.p., 1962), 76; Augusta B. Fothergill, Wills of Westmoreland County, Virginia, 1654-1800 (n.p.: Appeals Press, 1925), 39.

[3] Dorman, Westmoreland County, Virginia Order Books 1690-1698, Part II, 1692-1694 (Washington, D.C.: n.p., 1963), 67.

[4] Dorman, Westmoreland County Order Books, Part II, 1692-1694, 67; John Frederick Dorman, ed., "Prince William County, Virginia Order Book 1759-1761," The Virginia Genealogist, Vol. 20, No. 1, Jan.-March 1976, 41; Ruth and Sam Sparacio, comps., Virginia County

continued on next page

John Jarvis improved his social position by marrying Elizabeth Field, daughter of Abraham Field II of Westmoreland County. The Fields were a wealthy family from England. Elizabeth's grandfather, the first Abram Field, consorted with the Washington and Butler families. His early death in 1674, at about the age of 38, left his six children a good inheritance.

By 1710, John Jarvis and Elizabeth Field had married. Their children were John, Jane, Field, Eleanor, James, and Catherine. On October 25, 1710, John Jarvis, Elizabeth Jarvis, and Frances Field acknowledged a gift of land to their brother-in-law, David Rozier, Jr. Most likely, this land was a part of Abraham Field II's inheritance.[5]

A mystery regarding the early Jarvis family was the bequest left to James Jarvis, son of John and Elizabeth Field Jarvis. This James Jarvis disappeared from Westmoreland County records after September 1713. Neighbor James Vaulx, in his will dated October 16, 1710, carried out September 6, 1711, left James Jarvis a slave and some tobacco.[6] The mother of James Vaulx, Mary Bagge, left James Jarvis one slave and 2,000 pounds of tobacco on September 5, 1713.[7] One supposes that this was the same bequest.

Court Records--Stafford County, Virginia--Will Book (Liber 0) 12 July 1748-July Court 1767 (McLean, VA: Ruth and Sam Sparacio, n.d.), 50.

[5] Fothergill, 117; Oct. 25, 1710, Westmoreland Co. Order Books 1705-21; Ibid., 151.

[6] Fothergill, 51, 74-75.

[7] Fothergill, 51.

In 1712, John Jarvis was summoned to the West-moreland County Court over a dispute with physician John Wordon over ineffective medicine. The result was that Jarvis had to pay 600 pounds of tobacco. Jarvis later opposed a public road through his property, and the resulting petitions lasted for years. John died in 1744, and Elizabeth died by 1763.[8]

John, Jr., married and had six children: Thomas, Margery (m. Bartholomew Staton), Sarah, Elizabeth (m. Edward Vickers), John, and Joseph. John Jarvis, Jr., left Westmoreland for Amherst County, Virginia, after 1763, where he was mentioned in a land transaction. Succeeding generations of John's family settled in Rock-bridge County, Virginia.[9]

Another son of John and Elizabeth, Field Jarvis, died in 1765. Field left four young children, who re-mained unnamed in official records, but one was Field Jarvis, Jr. (1756-1839). The younger Field moved from

[8] Wordon v Jarvis, Westmoreland County Order Books 1705-21, N342 (Richmond, VA: VA State Library Photographic Lab, n.d.), 157A; Westmoreland County Order Books, 143-143A; Westmoreland County Deeds, No. 14, Posititve Reel 12, No. 4318, J102 (Richmond, VA: VA State Photo Library, n.d.), Frames 387-388; Fothergill, 117; Westmoreland County Deeds and Wills, No. 14, (Richmond, VA: VA State Library Photographic Lab, n.d.), 219-222.

[9] Hazel B. Lloyd, "A Virginia Family", Jarvis Family Notes, Vol. I, No. 3, Nov. 1971, (San Jose, CA: Rose Family Association, 1971), 70; Westmoreland County Deeds and Wills, No. 14 (Richmond, VA: VA State Photo Lab, n.d.), 219-222.

Westmoreland County in October 1773. It is likely that Field lived with his uncle for a time.[10]

In 1776, Field joined the Virginia Militia and served three months guarding lead mines in Wythe County, Virginia. Colonel Ennis of the militia discharged Field about the first of March 1777. He volunteered a second time from Bedford County, Virginia, in September 1777. Field marched through Prince Edward and Buckingham Counties to Little York (Yorktown), and then to Williamsburg. In 1781, he moved to Botetourt County, Virginia. Later, Field joined the Virginia Militia a third time to guard prisoners from New London to Lynchburg, Virginia.[11]

For military services to Virginia, Field was allotted a segment of land. From the sale of this land in 1792, he bought land in Monroe County. Pension certificate 16,095 awarded Field a pension of $21.11 a month from March 1831 until his death in 1839.[12]

The land Field bought was an entire valley. The valley contained Ewing's Run, which is a branch of Potts' Creek. The valley was rich in fertile soil, though there

---

[10] Westmoreland County Inventories and Settlements of Estates, No. 4 (filmed by the Genealogical Society of Utah, 1947), 214-214A; Field Jarvis Pension Record, Revolutionary War Pension and Bounty-Land Warrant and Application Files, Records of the Veterans Administration, Record Group 15 (hereafter referred to as "RG"), M804, Roll 1408, National Archives, Washington, D.C.

[11] Ibid.

[12] Ibid.; Jarvis to Gillispie, March 2, 1792, Deed Book DC, Monroe County Court House, 24-25.

was much rocky terrain. Through the years, parcels of this land reverted to relatives.[13]

In 1783, while the county was still known as Botetourt, Field married Asenith Adams. There is still a mystery as to where Asenith's family originated. Suffice it to say, there were several Adams families in Botetourt County.[14] *Field and Asenith Jarvis had an undetermined number of children. One of the oldest was Susanna (c. 1786--c. 1870), who married into the Linton family. Winnifred (c. 1795--c. 1850) was single in the 1850 Census and living with her brother. John Franklin Jarvis (1791-1870) was the most documented of the clan. Mary Ann (1788-1859) married into the Neel Family. The youngest known child was Field A. Jarvis (1800-1890).*[15]

---

[13] Morton, <u>History of Monroe County, West Virginia</u> (Baltimore, MD: Regional Publishing Co., 1980), map in front cover; Orville H. Bostic Interview by author, Fairfax, VA, October, 1988.

[14] Maggie Gray Pence lineage in National Society of the Daughters of the American Revolution Lineage Book, Volume 151, 150001-151000 (Washington, D.C.: n.p., 1936), 306-307; Charles T. Burton, comp., <u>Botetourt County, Virginia, Early Settlers</u>, (n.p., n.d.). Note: Early DAR lineage books may not be accurate.

[15] Norma Pontiff Evans, <u>Monroe County (West) Virginia Marriages: A Compiled List 1799-1850</u> (Beaumont, TX: Tony Reyes Printing, 1985), 20; Population Schedules of the Seventh Census--1850, RG29 M432, Roll 961, National Archives, Washington, D.C.; Jack Bostic and Layman Reynolds, comps., Bostic Cemetery Listing, New Castle, VA, 1988, no. 55; Morton, <u>Monroe</u>, 384.

Asenith died sometime after the 1820 Census, but before the 1830 one. Any slaves the Jarvis family might have owned were freed after 1820. John accumulated several land grants in Monroe County. An 1822 indenture included 617 acres along Ewing's Run.[16]
Field A. Jarvis married Sally Ervin of Alleghany County. Their children were to figure prominently in the Unionist activity that followed. They were: Mary Ann W. (1832-1923), known as "Winnie"; Asenith M. (1835-1923), known as "Tillie"; Jane R. (1836-1927); John E. (1839-1907); Joseph M. (1842-1927); Morgan T. (1847-1865); and Virginia (1851-1921).[17]
John served as an ensign in the Virginia Militia. He had at least five children, according to the records: Nancy, Mary S., William, and Washington Jarvis. Washington, also known as "Wash" Jarvis, was a Justice

---

[16] Population Schedules of the Fourth Census of the United States--1820, RG29, M33, Roll 133, National Archives, Washington, D.C.; Population Schedules of the Fifth Census--1830, RG29, M19, Roll 198, National Archives, Washington, DC.; State of West Virginia, Land Department, State Auditor's Office, Sims Index to Land Grants in West Virginia (Charleston, WV: Rose City Press, 1952), 524.

[17] Declaration of Original Pension of a Father--Field A. Jarvis Pension Record dated Nov. 21, 1878, No. 240535, RG15, Records of the Veterans Administration, National Archives, Washington, D.C.; Bostic Cemetery--Bostic and Reynolds; Virginia Wilson grave, Glenwood Cemetery, Washington, D.C.; Final Pay Voucher, in John E. Jarvis Pension 695530, RG15, National Archives, Washington, D.C.

of the Peace and Juror in Monroe County during the Civil War.[18]

As families grew, the valley filled with settlers. Most were relations of the families of Linton, Rose, Armentrout, Bostic, Crosier, and Smith. These families, like the Jarvis family, had moderate means and strong nationalistic fiber and beliefs. While these farmers made their living, the country was close to a civil war.

---

[18] Morton, <u>Monroe</u>, 268; Ibid., 466; Bostic, Interview, Oct. 1988.

WHAT THE WAR DID

The American Civil War tore many families apart. Monroe County was, at first, Unionist, but when Virginia seceded from the Union on April 17, 1861, Monroe, with tension growing, became secessionist. Even so, many citizens remained loyal to the United States. Some citizens, such as John Goode of Craig County, hired speakers to promote the Unionist element. Most hid their sympathies, waiting for a quick outcome.[1]

The struggle was not easily resolved. Many in Monroe County soon realized the Civil War was to be a personal war, striking deep into the hearts of the farmer, the blacksmith, and the editor. Monroe had abundant supplies of food, men, and horses, but this did not ease the internal conflicts of what the people believed. Much had to do with geography and occupation. Monroe was a county with valley farmers and mountain farmers, and the sympathies of Monroe families followed these separate social lines.

We must realize that these people were Southerners. They invested in some beliefs that the Confederacy stood for, and valley and mountain farmers alike sought state and local rights. Some believed in the institution of slavery as it existed, though many did not. Many of the

---

[1]Southern Claims Commission File Claim 8218, Question No. 40, RG123, National Archives, Washington, D.C. (Hereafter known as SCC)

mountain farmers disagreed with the issue of secession from the United States Government entirely since most had no need for slaves and disliked the rich secessionist tidewater planters. The mountain farmers wished to raise their families in peace. Although some of the mountain farmers found this impossible in the political climate of Monroe County, they found ways to resist the effects of the War. It was not the Southern heritage they disdained, but the underlying planter logic.

The Jarvis family and their neighbors were mountain farmers. They viewed the War primarily as a disruption of their daily lives. Field A. Jarvis labored as both a farmer and blacksmith. Winnie and Tillie, two of his older daughters, never married and stayed with him. His son Joseph, a hunchbacked man with a notably bad temper, also lived there. In 1861, the Field A. Jarvis family was unreconciled to the idea of the Confederacy.[2]

Many in Monroe, Craig, and Alleghany counties had strong Confederate sympathies. By July 1861, Monroe soldiers participated in the Battle of First Manassas. Most served in the famous Stonewall Brigade. These men, under Captain Hugh Tiffany, were among the first in western Virginia to fight in the Civil War and, along with Hugh Tiffany, to perish in the battle.[3] Local ora-

---

[2]Bostic Interview by author, June, 1989.

[3]Jim Comstock, ed., West Virginia Heritage Encyclopedia, Volume 1-Supplemental Series (Richwood, WV: Jim Comstock, 1974), 71-72; Samuel Rutherford Houston, "A War Diary" in History of Monroe County, West Virginia by Oren F. Morton (Baltimore: Regional Publishing, 1980), July 24, 1861, 171.

tors and politicians such as Allen Taylor Caperton and Augustus Alexandria Chapman spoke out with force. Caperton even sought a seat and became a member of the Confederate Congress. From his home "Elmwood," in the town of Union, Caperton became a community and Southern leader.[4]

Monroe County was out of the Union's reach until late summer, 1861: Manassas had made a Federal victory critical for their cause. Lincoln looked to both western Virginia and Missouri for such a victory. Federal officer George McClellan advanced with his Ohio troops and temporarily ended any threat to the Baltimore & Ohio Railroad.[5]

On June 3rd, 1861, McClellan's troops surprised Colonel George Porterfield's Virginians at Philippi, in Barbour County. The Confederates, who had been caught sleeping without an adequate picket, fled in panic. The lines moved south and east, and U.S. Colonel Lew Wallace, with the 11th Indiana Infantry, raided Romney on June 13th. Union General Jacob Cox advanced to the town of Gauley Bridge.[6]

---

[4]Morton, Monroe, S.R. Houston Diary, 166; Ibid., 169; Morton, Monroe, 323.

[5]Jacob D. Cox, "McClellan in West Virginia" in Alfred A. Nofi, ed., Eyewitness to the Civil War, volume I, The Opening Guns--Fort Sumter to Bull Run, 1861 (New York: Combined Books, 1988), 135.

[6]Cox, "McClellan in West Virginia" in Nofi, ed., Opening Guns, 135; Stan Cohen, The Civil War in West Virginia (Charleston, WV: Pictorial Histories Publishing Co., 1976), 23; Ibid., 26; Tim McKinney, Robert E. Lee

continued on next page

3

The events at Romney, Philippi, and Gauley Bridge frightened the citizens of Monroe, Craig, and Alleghany Counties. Rumors sent zealous citizens to meet the enemy with all manner of weaponry, even farming , tools. Most of these were false alarms, particularly in Monroe County. However, it prepared the population for war. The 19th Brigade, Virginia Militia, was organized by Confederate General Augustus A. Chapman to defend that part of the state. Of the 19th Brigade units, Monroe County's 108th Virginia Militia[7] was among the oldest of regiments. It began service in 1794. Until 1861, the 108th was more of a social club than a military unit and met for little more than annual parties. Come the Civil War, the 108th was to see fighting.[8]

Some men of Monroe fought in a unit of the "Stonewall Brigade," the 27th Virginia Infantry. William Tristam Patton served with this unit and, later, as an officer in Chapman's Battery. Several, like the aforementioned Captain Hugh Tiffany, never returned to Monroe.[9]

Unionists and reluctant Southern sympathizers hesitated, most preferring to wait and watch Lincoln's reaction. Manassas acted as a tonic for the South, and

---

at Sewell Mountain (Charleston, WV: Pictorial Histories Publishing Company, 1990), iii.

[7]Lee A. Wallace, Jr., A Guide to Virginia Military Organizations 1861-1865 (Lynchburg, VA: H.E. Howard, Inc., 1986), 271; Morton, Monroe, 152; for a full list of members of the 108th, see appendix.

[8]Morton, Monroe, 152, 264.

[9]Comstock, ed., West Virginia Heritage Encyclopedia, 71; J. L. Scott, Lowry's, Bryan's, and Chapman's Batteries, (Lynchburg: H. E. Howard, Inc., 1988), 103.

Alva Linton (left) and a member of the Rose family at ruins of Allen Armentrout's Mill. Courtesy of Alva Linton.

numbers of recruits jumped to enlist. Chapman easily filled the first ranks. Among the recruits were John E. Jarvis, Jackson Rose, William Smith, and Allen Armentrout. All four were Unionists and probably enlisted out of fear of being discovered as Unionists.[10]

Confederate Colonel John M. Rowan, commander of the 108th Virginia Militia, marched west to defend the Kanawha Valley. The commanding Confederate generals, John B. Floyd and Henry Wise, disliked each other so intensely that they spent more time trying to relieve the other of command than in facing their common foe. Wise and Floyd could not agree upon a position to fight the Ohio troops. Chapman and Confederate militia General Albert Beckley stayed with Wise. Floyd favored camps remote to Monroe. Chapman was primarily concerned about Monroe County's defense. While Wise stressed the importance of Gauley Bridge, Floyd camped further north, near Carnifex Ferry.[11]

---

[10] Confederate Roster Book, 108th Virginia Militia, No. 20, Virginia State Library, Richmond, VA, 180; Ibid, 187; Ibid, 193; Allen Armentrout Service Record, Item 17, Compiled Service Records of Confederate Soldiers who Served in Organizations from Virginia, RG 109, M324, Roll 1053, National Archives, Washington, D.C.

[11] Terry Lowry, September Blood--The Battle of Carnefex Ferry, (Charleston, WV: Pictorial Histories Publishing, 1985), 11; Rowan Service Record, Item 462A, RG109, M324, Roll 1053, National Archives; Henry Wise Report, Sept. 4, 1861, U.S. War Department, War of the Rebellion, A Compilation of the Official Records of the Union and Confederate Armies, 128 Volumes (Washington, D.C.: Government Printing

continued on next page

The escalating war had little to do with the Jarvis family, save the recruitment of John E. Jarvis. Life remained somewhat normal in an otherwise tempestuous environment. Jane became a school teacher in a oneroom school house along Forest Run, Virginia, where she stayed with the family of Jesse Bostic.[12] It was in Forest Run that Jane became acquainted with the Bostics and Parkers and later met her husband-to-be, James Alexander Bostic.

James Bostic was in the 108th Virginia Militia as was John E. Jarvis, though they served in different companies. Bostic was elected 2nd Lieutenant of his company, while John Jarvis remained a private. Their term of enlistment started August 3, 1861, and extended to October 13, 1861. Colonel Rowan led the regiment to Cotton Hill in Fayette County, where they participated in a sharp skirmish on September 3, 1861, against Cox's Federals in Gauley Bridge. Cox held, and the attack broke off at nightfall.[13]

Office, 1881-1901), Series 1, Volume 5, 123 (Hereafter referred to as OR).

[12] Confederate Roster Book, 180; Layman Reynolds interview by author, Keenan, West Virginia, Sept. 1991.

[13] Confederate Roster Book, 180; Ibid, 188; Compiled Service Records of Confederate Soldiers who Served in Organizations from the State of Virginia, War Department Collection of Confederate Records, RG109, M324, Roll 1053, National Archives, Washington, D.C.; Letters Received by the Confederate Secretary of War 1861-1865, RG109, M437, Roll 31, National Archives, Washington, D.C.; Henry Wise Report, Sept. 5, 1861, OR, Volume 5, 123.

The Confederates retreated from the region upon the arrival of Federal reinforcements. These men were General William Rosecrans' forces from Ohio. The hasty retreat was documented in a later letter by the Quartermaster of the 19th Brigade, Virginia Militia. Wise and Floyd argued constantly, but the arrival of the overall commander of forces in Virginia, General Robert E. Lee, steadied nerves and calmed some of the disagreements. The Confederates decided to maintain a defense at Meadow Bluff, Greenbrier County. In October, Lee granted the militia permission to return to their homes for the harvest, once they had cleared the roads south of Sewell Mountain.[14]

This was the only Confederate service of John E. Jarvis. The assault from Cotton Hill, futile as it was, disillusioned many, among them were John Jarvis' neighbors. Jackson Rose tried to desert twice at Cotton Hill and chose imprisonment rather than service in the Confederate Army when he was recalled in February of 1862.[15]

Environment and mindset were not the only factors. Certainly blood ties also played a part with making

---

[14] McKinney, Lee at Sewell Mountain, 93-94; Certification--Captain H.J. Kelly and Colonel John M. Rowan, April 23, 1862, Compiled Records of Confederate Soldiers from Virginia, RG109, M324, Roll 1053, National Archives, Washington, D.C.; Lee to Wise, OR, Vol. 5, 868.

[15] Confederate Roster Book; Col. John M. Rowan to Confederate Commissioner Sydney Baxter, dated Feb. 24, 1862, RG109, M437, Roll 31, National Archives, Washington, D.C.

7

the decision to stay with the Confederacy and its militia. The Jarvis family had relations in Gallia County, Ohio, and their cousins, the Glenn family of Gallia, had at least three sons in the Union forces.[16]

The Confederate militia, as it existed, affected all families. Alleghany County had its own militia, the 128th. With secession, the militia became a "home guard" and more of a police force. Craig County was the home of the 189th Virginia Militia. Many of those who made up this unit went on to fight in Confederate Colonel George S. Patton's 22nd Virginia Infantry. Craig County men were in the majority in Company C, the "Mountain Cove Guards." The leaders were local citizens of wealth and eminence, such as A. A. Chapman of Monroe and Thompson McAllister of Alleghany, a brother of General Robert McAllister of the Union forces.[17]

These Confederate officers were mainly longtime residents of the fertile valley regions of the three coun-

---

[16] Application for Gilbert W. Glenn Pension, no. 883415, Bureau of Pensions and the Veterans Administration, RG15, National Archives, Washington, D.C.; Ohio Roster Commission, Official Roster of the Soldiers of the State of Ohio 1861-1866, Vol. 9 (Cincinnati: Ohio Valley Press, 1889), 606.

[17] Wallace, Guide to Virginia Military Organizations, 274; Lowry, 22nd Virginia Infantry (Lynchburg, VA: H.E. Howard, Inc., 1988) 103-104; Oren T. Morton, A Centennial History of Alleghany County (Harrisonburg, VA: reprint by C.J. Carrier Co., 1986), 44 [originially published by J.K. Ruebush Co., 1923]; W.M. McAllister, "Alleghany Roughs, or Carpenter's Battery," in Confederate Veteran, Volume XIII, No. 8, August 1905 (Wendell, NC: Broadfoot's Bookmark reprint), 366.

ties. Thompson McAllister was a notable exception. Coming from Adams County, Pennsylvania, he migrated to Alleghany to invest in local business. The Chapmans, Capertons, Carpenters, and others were people with much of their wealth invested in the community.[18]

The second contingent of people were the poor mountain farmers. They comprised most of the populace in the three counties. They harvested their crops and grew what they needed to eat or barter. Most of them cared little about the slave question and less for the rich planters hovering about the county seat. They did not wish to fight for anyone and, often, would resist to keep from fighting.

The last class of people in this area were the Unionists. These men never believed in the Confederacy, or, if they did, believed primary loyalty should be to the Union. Unlike the mountain farmer pacifist, the Unionist was not always willing to engage the Confederates. More likely, they fought back by small, often individual, means. There were secret societies that conducted meetings and worked for the Union. They often harbored fugitives from the local police and militia. They supplied food to passing Union troops, and, at times, they were involved in bushwhacking, especially if one of their own was a prisoner.

Unionists and pacifists were often mistaken for one another. However, alliances were made, and some of one contingent sided with the other. Shade was often so subtle that sometimes one could not tell one group from another.

---

[18] Morton, Alleghany, 132.

Which category included the Jarvis family? The Rose family? The Ballard family? Why focus on one family? The Jarvis family was diverse, having members in each group. The following is not simply a case study of one family; it is a study of three counties. The focal point of the study centers on a typical western Virginia family. This work does not ignore the important events of the War, but emphasizes those events that directly affected the inhabitants of these counties.

Chapter One

THE OPENING YEAR--1861

Although secession appeared at first soundly defeated, the rich valley farmers and planters brought Monroe County into alliance with the Confederacy. The town of Union bristled with activity, as attested to by the Reverend S.R. Houston, who noted many orations advocating secession by prominent persons as early as November 1860. Major John Echols, Allen Taylor Caperton, and Augustus Alexandria Chapman were among such people.[1]

Houston, a Presbyterian Minister, became a cautious secessionist. His diary was staunchly conservative at first and spoke little of secession, but as time progressed, Houston began to change his views. Although the Deep South (Florida, South Carolina, Mississippi, Georgia, Louisiana, and Alabama) had seceded by February, 1861, Lincoln was still in favor with the people of Monroe County. Houston, among others, was hopeful of the "spirit" brought by Lincoln's inaugural ceremonies. By March 6, however, Houston decided it was "warlike."[2]

Although the Unionists, in an attempt to persuade people to remain in the Union, also instituted public speaking activities, Monroe had few true Unionists. Sev-

---

[1] Morton, Monroe, S.R. Houston Diary, Nov. 19, 1860, 166, January 20, 1861, 167.

[2] Ibid, March 4 and 6, 1861, 167; Morton, Monroe, 358.

eral groups of Unionists were the Ballards in Greenville and several families near Waiteville. John Goode, of Abbott in Craig County, aided in the promotion of Constitutional Unionists like William Anthony as they spoke at places such as New Castle (Craig Court House). Alleghany County remained quiet, however, as local Unionists were confined to the southern portion of the County, and, more specifically, to Potts' Creek and its tributaries. As this area was geographically separate from Covington, Secessionists held sway in Alleghany.[3]

The mountain farmer had the hardest lot of all in that he owned no great acreage or slaves. He and his family toiled at their small farms to produce what little they lived on. A core of mountain farmers, a common strand of Unionist sentiment, ran through all three counties. Most were indifferent, or mildly interested, in the trouble around them, as long as their life was not affected. The Abraham Armentrout family kept their mill running near Paint Bank. Henry Tingler worked in that same occupation. Field A. Jarvis worked as a blacksmith, and had a few livestock animals grazing in the yard. These were the men, among others, who would comprise the Unionist element as the War came.[4]

---

[3] Morton, <u>Monroe</u>, 305; SCC Claim--John Goode, RG 123, Court of Claims Records, NARA, Suitland, MD; Ibid., Question 40, John Goode Testimony, Sept. 9, 1872; Morton, <u>Alleghany</u>, 50.

[4] Question 24 in Henry Tingler, SCC File 5006, RG 233, M1407, fishe 3221, National Archives, Washington, D.C.; Bostic Interview, April 1990; Layman Reynolds Interview, Sept. 1991.

Then there were the Secessionists. While Chapman and Echols gave speeches at Union, others prepared to fight those who opposed the South. Nicholas Augustus Dunbar, a nephew of Field A. Jarvis by his sister Nancy, was one of the first to join the newly formed Bryan's Battery. In what would be Paint Bank, Allen Caperton Rowan, a relative of John M. Rowan of Gap Mills, formed his own company of local militia. He was to become a Lieutenant in George S. Patton's 22nd Virginia Infantry. Nearby lived Gibbons G. Figgatt, the son of Thomas A. and Jane Figgatt, who was to become a state militia officer in the popular 108th.[5]

In early 1861, young Smith Humphries of Alleghany County ventured to the Jarvis home. Smith lived close to Field's brother-in-law, Joseph Ervine. He planned to ask Field Jarvis' permission to marry his daughter Jane. There was no reason for Humphries not to feel confident.[6]

Field gave no objection when asked; but, Humphries had not counted on the resolve of Jane Jarvis, a short and direct woman. Humphries approached Jane, who, when asked, only glanced at the black clouds on the horizon. "You don't intend to marry me, do you, Miss

---

[5] N.A. Dunbar, Confederate Veteran, Vol. XXXIII, No. 5 (Wilmington, NC: reprint by Broadfoot Publishing, 1987), 187 [originally published by the Trustees of Confederate Veterans]; Bostic Interview, April 1990; Lowry, 22nd Virginia Infantry, 190; Monroe County, VA Population Schedules of the Eighth Census, RG29, T7, Roll 298, National Archives, Washington, D.C.; Confederate Roster Book.

[6] Ruby B. Linton Interview by author, Clifton Forge, VA, Sept. 1991.

Jarvis?" Humphries asked. "No, I do not," was the reply. "Well, you may not marry me, but one day you'll rue it!" was the angry reaction from Humprhies, but Jane repeated her intentions not to wed Humphries.[7]

Those clouds foreshadowed an entire war. The spring 1861 was filled with tension and Southern Nationalism. The former Southern Whigs were still in control of the state. The non-political mountain yeoman farmers reacted cautiously to the bombing of Fort Sumter. Virginia voted to stay within an undefined Union. Courthouse speeches took a new fevered pitch, exhorting anger at the aggressive nature that Lincoln's administration employed.

This would not last long. On April 18, 1861, Virginia seceded. The Virginia Convention had changed its mind from the decision made only a month earlier. Lincoln himself had tipped the balance. In a hope that the rebellion could be confined to a limited number of Southern states, Lincoln made a massive call for troops from each state still within the Union. Virginia was not willing to fight their fellow Southerners. In reaction to this, many moderate Virginians became the advocates of secession. The tone expressed at the state conventions and resulting reaction kept the remaining Unionists from further vocal activity. It was a dangerous time to back Lincoln.[8]

The three months of largely-psychological warfare in the region gave new life to the courthouse speeches of Chapman, Echols, and Caperton. The voice of secession

---

[7] Ibid.

[8] Morton, <u>Monroe</u>, March 18, 1861, 168.

14

was loud and clear in Monroe. The same sentiment swept through Craig Court House and Covington. The three counties were closer to lands loyal to the Union than not and were separated from their fellow Southerners by the Alleghany Mountains. For these reasons, the counties were more susceptible to invasion. As a result, new companies and county militia units began to drill in earnest.

The region had much to protect since a major road and mail distribution route, the James River and Kanawha Turnpike, ran right through it. The mountains made canal travel difficult, so the Turnpike was the main thoroughfare. The Salt Sulphur and Mountain Lake Turnpike, operated by Salt Sulphur Hotel owner William Erskine, was another main road. Still, the Virginia and Tennessee Railroad was the most important road in the region. The Virginia and Tennessee Railroad connected the two states and served to transport troops of the Confederacy. The depot town of Dublin, in Pulaski County, was used as a supply and command post in the area. Many Unionists were brought there to stand trial in the first months of the war. Local troops arrested John Webb of Craig County. Webb was taken to Dublin and placed in a dark cell where he caught a chill and later died.[9]

---

[9] Alex L. ter Brakke, "Postal History of the James River and Kanawha Turnpike," West Virginia History, Vol. XXXIII, No. 1, Oct. 1971 (Charleston, WV: WV State Department of Archives and History), 39 [originally from American Philatelic Congress Book, Vol. 36, Oct. 1970, 31-52]; Form on William Erskine, Confederate Papers Relating to Citizens or Business Firms, RG109,

In the place that would be called Paint Bank, a small village developed just within the border of Craig County. It was situated along Potts' Creek, and was 26 miles southwest of the Jackson River. The proximity of the village to the spas at Sweet Springs assured a solid settlement. The Lewis family of Lindside, owners of the Springs, were successful in establishing a community there. Other people did the same, and land sold well near the Springs. Abraham Armentrout, for example, bought 28 acres in 1846 and another 200 acres in 1851. Other families married into land-holding clans. John Barton Linton already had inherited land from his parents. Linton married Susannah Jarvis and, thus, a share of the family land. By the time John Linton died, on November 5, 1839, his widow retained only two horses and a trundle bed. Their children, among them George A. and James N. Linton, lived in the homes of their Jarvis kin. This arrangement depicted how families stuck together. Here, survival was the only thought, and families were extended families in their concern and aid.[10]

M346, Roll 286, National Archives, Washington, D.C.; Morton, Monroe, 207; Question 40, John Goode Testimony, SCC Claim, National Archives, Washington, D.C.; Cohen, The Civil War in West Virginia, 103; Howard Rollins McManus, The Battle of Cloyds Mountain--The Virginia and Tennessee Railroad Raid--April 29-May 19, 1864 (Lynchburg, VA: H.E. Howard, Inc., 1989), 2.

[10] Notice of Post Office Dept., Topographer's Office, dated Nov. 9, 1898, Post Office Department Report of Site Locations 1837-1950, RG28, M1126, Roll 607, National Archives, Washington, D.C.; John Lewis Inventory, 1823, Alleghany County Wills and Inventories

In neighboring Alleghany County in spring 1861, Michael Arritt Armentrout decided that he did not wish to fight against his home state. He did not want to fight for it either. As a result, Armentrout went through the lines and to Ohio. Many residents chose relocation rather than risking a loss in the family.[11]

For those who did decide to fight, the local militia system became a primary means. Monroe had the 166th and 108th militia units, Craig County had the smaller 189th militia. Alleghany was the home of the 128th Virginia Militia. The 189th was under the command of Lt. Col. (later Assistant Adjutant to General Henry Heth) William W. Finney. A. A. Chapman had the overall command of the 19th Brigade, which contained Giles County's 86th Virginia Militia, Mercer County's 151st, the 108th and 166th, the town of Union's 2nd Class Militia, and Greenbrier County's 79th. This fighting force would be called on many times during the summer and autumn of 1861.[12]

No. 1 1822-1837, (Richmond, VA: Genealogical Society of Utah, JR 2867, 1953), 22-23; Bostic Interview, Oct. 1988; State Auditor's Office of West Virginia, Sims Index, 514; Evans, Monroe County (West) Virginia Marriages, 20; Works Progress Administration, Monroe County, West Virginia, Vol. 3, Wills and Inventory (Washington, D.C.: typewritten, 1936), 16; Ibid., 41; James N. Linton, Monroe County, 1860 Census, RG29, M653, Roll 1363, National Archives, Washington, D.C.

[11] Louise C. Perkins, Wolf Family History Group Sheets (Sunbury, NC: n.p., 1992), No. 2702.

[12] Wallace, Guide to Virginia Military Organizations, 271-272; Ibid., 274; Ibid., 278; OR, Series I, Vol. 12, Part I, 493.

The indecisive period lasted months. Those west of the mountains expected to see the Federal troops at any time, and false alarms were not uncommon. One frightened solder-to-be, having second thoughts, decided to hide in a hollowed-out tree. To his amazement, he found someone else already occupying it.[13]

In mid-July 1861, a company of soldiers who had joined General Thomas J. Jackson's 27th Virginia Infantry fought at Manassas, where the General gained the nickname of "Stonewall." The battle cost the lives of many Monroe soldiers. Among those killed were Captain Hugh Tiffany, Wyley Wingfield, Robert Camp, John Conner, Robert Hamilton, Davidson Shanklin, Archibald Campbell, and Doctor John Patton. The Confederate forces won, and the residents of the region knew the arrival of war was simply a matter of time.[14]

It was. Union forces worked their way across the Ohio River. Soon after the Battle of Philippi, General Jacob Dolson Cox forced his way past Charleston and up the Great Kanawha River to the town of Gauley Bridge. The memory of Manassas was very far away.[15]

The events preceding Robert E. Lee's arrival moved quickly. On August 3, 1861, Monroe's 108th responded to the first roll call. Among its complement was 2nd Lieutenant James A. Bostic. Bostic was of mountain farmer stock on his father's side, and more gentleman farmer on his mother's. His maternal grandfather, James Parker, was the son of an Irish immigrant. Thus, while

---

[13] Morton, Monroe, 152.

[14] Comstock, Encyclopedia of West Virginia History, 71.

[15] McKinney, Sewell Mountain. iii.

James was not wealthy, he was well-to-do and adventurous.[16]

The first lieutenant in the same company as Bostic was Henderson Reed, a man of the same Forest Run neighborhood. The Reeds were loyal to old Virginia. These families also represented the mountain yeoman farmer who stood by the Confederate standard no matter what the personal cost.[17] Colonel John M. Rowan, commander of the 108th, did not fit any pattern that was typical of mountain yeoman farmers. He lived in the wealthy Sweet Springs Valley. It is, therefore, not surprising that Rowan led the regiment.[18]

Other units followed this pattern so that, where the wealthy were leading, the yeoman farmers were following. The South maintained the class system even in the military establishments. There were few exceptions. This situation explained some of the forthcoming bitterness in those who still had doubts over secession.

Floyd knew the Federals were coming and called on Wise for reinforcements. After being sent to the

---

[16] Frame 57, Compiled Service Records--Virginia, RG109, M324, Roll 1053, National Archives, Washington, D.C.; Bostic Interview, Oct. 1988; James Parker Will, June 1819, Will Book No. 2, Monroe County Court House, Union, WV, 1.

[17] Henderson Reed Service Record, Frame 445, Compiled Service Records--Virginia, RG109, M324, Roll 1053, National Archives, Washington, D.C.; Benjamin Reed Will, August 20, 1863, Will Book 10, Monroe County Court House, Union, WV, 13.

[18] Wallace, Virginia Military Organizations, 271; Morton, Monroe, 397-398.

Kanawha Valley, Chapman's Militia began to show signs of strain in its own solidarity. Private Jackson Rose tried to desert while stationed in Fayette County. Rose, an older man, almost 45, had never believed in the right of a state to secede. He stated his belief that the Federals would invade the territory in weeks. He had several young children to feed, and this precipitated his talk. Rose lived in an area that was consistently non-conformist. This was the community that would become Paint Bank. In his neighborhood resided none other than the aforementioned Field A. Jarvis. Rose did not have a chance, and soon he was captured. General Chapman spoke at some length with him, and Rose promised never to try desertion again. But this was only the beginning.[19]

On September 10th, Floyd battled Federal troops under General William S. Rosecrans at Carnefex Ferry. Wise had sent Colonel George Patton's 22nd Virginia, but no further aid. It drove Floyd to abandon his position.[20]

General Chapman's Militia left their forward position at Fayetteville and retreated westward. On the 15th of September, General Floyd received a letter from Chapman, stating the morale was so poor, many of the

---

[19] Col. John Rowan to Judge Boteler, Feb. 24, 1862, Confederate Secretary of War Letters Received, RG109, M437, Roll 31, National Archives, Washington, D.C.; Ibid, Gen. A.A. Chapman to Sydney Baxter, Feb. 12, 1862; Bostic Interview, October 1988; David S. Turk, "Mysterious Death of Southern Unionist," Rose Family Bulletin, Vol. XXIV, No. 95, September 1989, 3433-3436; Field A. Jarvis and Jackson Rose, Monroe County, 1860 Census, RG29, M653, National Archives.

[20] McKinney, Sewell Mountain, 17-18.

militia simply wanted to go home. The critical phase of the campaign was over.[21]

Meanwhile, local authorites in Monroe County had organized into patrols as early as May. Order books from the county clarified the meaning of these early police patrols. Concerned citizens worried about potential problems with local Unionists. On May 20, 1861, Gap Mills appointed a patrol headed by Captain Irvine B. Hull. Hull's patrol officers were Allen G. Neel, William P. Denaux, Thomas Teas, A.I. Humphreys, J.A.I. Hull and William Hastings. The town of Rocky Point and Andrew Beirne's Lewis Place region had organized patrols. Supply relief for area families divided within the county to seven distinct districts. All districts were under the general agency of James Byrnside. County Clerk George W. Hutchinson became the agent for disbursing and borrowing needed funds. The County of Monroe paid volunteer musicians $1.50 a day for ten days in May 1861.[22]

As the environment in Monroe County was so controlled, there were fewer chances for insurgents to get a foothold. For obvious reasons, Unionists stayed clear of county-appointed patrols. Many of the later Unionist, like Jackson Rose, were already in the volunteer units and away from the county. In the Paint Bank community, most were serving in Captain Gibbons Figgatt's company in the 108th. Locally, many of the Unionists

---

[21] Ibid., 23.

[22] Monroe County Order Book No. 8, May 20th, 1861, 256; Ibid, 266; Morton, Monroe, 159.

had other concerns. For example, Field A. Jarvis was suffering from a protracted attack of typhoid fever.[23] Alleghany County, because much of it is mountainous terrain, was hard to control. A Committee of Safety increased centralized control in 1863, when the war actually came within its boundaries. Craig County was little different, with its mixture of hill country and windy hollows. Craig Court House did not produce the effective controls Monroe had in the war's early stages, but these patrols would improve steadily as the war continued.[24]

To the west, the troops tired of the fight. The morale was not good, and the Federals were in better winter quarters. Lee's reputation was suffering due to incessant road repair work and the trench digging in which most of the troops participated. Another imposed strain on the doubtful Unionists pushed them further toward action. Now the Confederacy asked for their boys, their homes, and their food. There was no end to the hardship.[25]

Lee dismissed the militia upon the completion of cleansing a portion of the James and Kanawha Turnpike of debris and damage, by October 13th. In November,

---

[23] Confederate Roster Book, Vol. 20, Virginia State Library, 185; Ibid, 193; W.G. Cook Testimony, Summary of Material Facts dated June 22, 1879, Field A. Jarvis Pension, RG15, National Archives, Washington, D.C.

[24] Morton, Alleghany, 54.

[25] David Phillips, ed., "The Richmond Light Infantry Blues" in War Stories: Civil War in West Virginia (Leesburg, VA: Gauley Mount Press, 1991), 297. [From Barton H. Wise, The Life of Henry A. Wise].

Floyd's extended position on Cotton Hill was almost trapped by the Federals. Eventually, Floyd dropped back.[26]

If anything was important about the Kanawha Campaign, it was the lack of efficiency. Captain Henry J. Kelly certified that 109 bags of provisions disappeared during the retreat of the 108th Militia in October. Colonel John M. Rowan stated,

> ...[I] do certify that we were connected with the 19th Brigade Va. Ma. under the command of Brig. Genl. AA Chapman during the months of Aug Sept & Octo last and from our knowledge & observation with regard to the difficulties & embarrassing circumstances under which said march was made...[27]

"Embarrassing" was the key word. The management and conditions of the Confederate defense were appalling. It was no minor miracle that the weather and an inefficient union supply line saved them.

With the campaign over, but the Federals not so far away, conditions in Monroe County continued to worsen. In October, Lewis Ballard of Greenville was indicted by the Commonwealth of Virginia. The charge was for instigating others to establish a usurped government. Ballard's brother Jeremiah was also charged.

---

[26] McKinney, Sewell Mountain, 93-94, 113.

[27] Certification of Capt. H.J. Kelly and Col. John M. Rowan, April 23, 1862, RG109, M324, Roll 1053, National Archives.

They were both fined $1,000, although they vehemently denied the charges.[28]

William Smith, a friend of Jackson Rose and a soldier in Gibbons Figgatt's unit in the 108th, was also charged with the same crime.

> ...the Deft. pleads not guilty to the indict-
> ment puts himself upon the Country & the
> allo. to the Commonwealth likewise, and
> for reasons the next quarterly term....[29]

Smith was fined $500 and ordered to appear on November 1, 1861.[30]

This signified Unionist activity in the region was increasing. There was still doubt that any formal groups with hardened purpose, other than resistance to the patrols, actually existed at this time. There was the possibility that Constitutional Unionists, who never wanted secession in the first place, were encouraged by the advance of Cox's force. Ballard had voted against secession. Smith and Rose aroused suspicion of disloyal activity. Public disdain was the reward.[31]

---

[28] Monroe Order Book 8, 296-297; Morton, Monroe, 160.

[29] Monroe Order Book 8, 297.

[30] Ibid.

[31] Margaret B. Ballard, William Ballard--A Genealogical Record of his Descendants in Monroe County (Baltimore, MD: Pridemark Press, 1957), 250; Sidney S. Baxter, March 15, 1862, RG109, Letters Received by the Confederate Secretary of War, M437, Roll 31, National Archives.

In what was to become Paint Bank, the major concern of the winter of 1861-62 was the realignment of the public highway along Potts' Creek. Mason V. Hellems, John S. Cale, and William Baker were all appointed as Commissioners to align the road through the lands of Frances Rowan. The Commission broke the Rowan tract into lots. Road improvement was urgent for troop movement in the spring.[32]

When James Bostic returned from the 108th to his home in October, he met Jane Richardson Jarvis. Jane was a school teacher in the Forest Run community. She was boarding with a family of Bostics. "He was six-foot tall and handsome, or at least I thought so," Jane said later to her grandchildren.[33]

James and Jane married on Christmas Day, 1861. Even then, the war made itself known. The wedding took place in the home of James' maternal relatives, the Parker family. While the ceremony was in process, several of the local police patrol entered the house. One was a man by the name of Ryder, from Pocohontas County. Other patrolmen were Napoleon Patton, a Beane relative and an Eggleston. Apparently, there was concern that James would not rejoin the Confederate Army. In any case, the patrolmen quickly ended the intrusion, and the wedding was allowed to continue.[34]

Such activity proved the tight social controls Monroe County had by the end of 1861. Precious little resis-

---

[32] Craig County Order Book 2, 1860-63, Positive Reel 5, No. JR2880, New Castle, VA: Genealogical Society of Utah, 1953, 40, Virginia State Archives, Richmond, VA.

[33] Mrs. Ruby Linton Interview, Sept., 1991.

[34] Mr. Laymon Reynolds Interview, Sept., 1991.

tance could survive, even if it was passive resistance. Only in the mountainous regions of Alleghany and Craig would some hardened resistance eventually appear. In the meantime, the quest to root out the union men continued, as when spring came, so would the Yankees.

Jane Richardson Jarvis about 1927. Courtesy of Ruby Bostic Linton.

CHAPTER TWO

SOUTHERN PENDULUM--1862

The autumn of 1861 represented the first of four critical periods in the Alleghany-Monroe-Craig region. The first critical period was the Kanawha Valley Campaign. In May 1862, the advance of the Federals to Greenbrier County was imminent. This phase continued until that autumn, when Confederate General William Wing Loring captured Charleston. The second critical stage, was foretold by events within Monroe County.

Monroe County and area Unionists had to feel satisfaction. Confederate forces proved to be ineffectual under Floyd and Wise, and the Federals were close. However, the Unionists did not count on the backlash of county support for the Confederates. Whether a "Unionist" was a loyal Southerner who questioned the validity of secession was no longer the crucial issue. The war was too close, the local power figures sensitive to any criticism of their efforts, and the civilians were too fearful. It likened itself to a negative reaction first felt by Southerners following John Brown's Harper's Ferry Raid in which Brown attempted to lead a slave-uprising. One hundred and sixteen Monroe citizens petitioned the Confederate Secretary of War in Richmond to "ask that early and efficient means be taken to render their Country safe from the threatened invasion." Whether or not coerced to sign, the names of Unionists Frank Neel and Baldwin Ballard were on the same petition.[1]

Richmond was slow to respond to pleas of help from Monroe County. Monroe County citizens took local matters into their own hands. General Chapman called on a portion of the militia to guard the road into the county near Pack's Ferry. Confederate Captain Washington Lemons's Company, of the 108th Militia, was mustered for service at Pack's Ferry. Chapman wrote,

> I certify that in the month of Jan. 1862 my brigade was invaded by the enemy and that I called out for the defense of said Brigade, a portion of the 108th Regiment, and the company commanded by Capt. Washington Lemons--was in the service for the time stated in the annexed roll which upon examination I find to be correct.[2]

Anxious Civilians were also apparent on the Union side. Some private citizens of Monroe County were instrumental in the cause of Unionism. In late 1861, David Noble crossed beyond the lines into Federally-occupied territory. Thomas Sexton, an older man, took several journeys across the lines to transport correspondence between Noble and his parents. The inflammatory letters

---

[1] Various Letters from Citizens of Monroe County, Letters Received by Confederate Secretary of War, RG109, M437, Roll 60, National Archives.

[2] Company C Muster Roll, Jan. 1 to Feb. 10, 1862, 108th Virginia Militia, RG109, M324, Roll 1053, National Archives.

Sexton brought back from Noble put them at risk. Noble had not only left Monroe, but joined the 8th Regiment, Virginia Volunteers, U.S. Army. Written on the 1st of January, 1862, the letter proved to be a bombshell that would launch the latest flurry of citizen arrests.[3]

I heard from you all yesterday from Mr. Sexton...Father you have no idea the Joy it gave me to hear you was a <u>Union</u> man for it has give me a many hours uneasyness to know if you had seceeded from this glorious government--that oure fore fathers had so valiantly fought to sustain...Father against son and son against the father and Brother aginst against brother...I am sorrow to know that Joseph is one of the enemy <u>but</u> I wish well in evry respect as to health and safety.[4]

Noble's spirits were high. He wrote to tell his father that "we will wave our flag in Union and White Sulphur before the first day of April. We got Forty Eight Thousand troops ready to march...."[5] Words such as these provided fuel to an already fearful citizenry.

Witnesses proclaimed that Sexton, as a result of his role in delivery, was a fervent Union man and dangerous to the Confederate cause. Goodall Garten stated, "I heard him say (that is said Thomas Sexton) that he was a Union man & always has been...." Merit Collins claimed that Sexton spoke of trips to Unionist Kanawha

---

[3] David Noble to Father, Jan. 1, 1862, RG109, M437, Roll 31, National Archives.

[4] Ibid.

[5] Ibid.

29

County. Collins also stated that Sexton had bragged to taking the Oath to the United States. John Clarke heard Sexton say that he was a full-blooded abolitionist. Clarke added that Sexton wanted to go back to Kanawha County in 10 or 15 days. Whether or not this testimony was realistic, Sexton was arrested for disloyalty on February 3rd.[6]

The arrests took on a greater dimension. S.R. Houston noted in his diary "January 6--A prominent citizen named Landcraft on New River apprehended for harboring the Yankee and giving them counsel. He is to be tried at Red Sulphur Springs today."[7] John Echols, now a Confederate Colonel, gave another stirring speech on Court Day (January 20), undoubtedly giving the county a military feel. A controlled police-state environment was developing.[8]

Jackson Rose abhorred the patrols. He unwisely told a neighbor that he was involved with a group of men from Alleghany and Monroe Counties that would "rise and resist" any attempt to force them into the Confederate militia. Rose's statement was the first noted mention of any organized group of Unionists in the area. Rose said he felt the South would get a whipping and that the Federals would soon be there. These were dangerous words

---

[6] Lt. Col. G.W.H. Nickell Report, Feb. 3, 1862, RG109, M437, Roll 31, National Archives.

[7] Morton, S.R. Houston Diary, Monroe, Jan. 6, 1862, 173.

[8] Ibid., Jan. 20, 1862.

spoken at a sensitive time, and the punishment for them was severe.[9]

Word of Rose's statements reached the local authorities in Monroe County, and an armed patrol rode out to arrest Rose. One of Rose's younger sons, Harvey Brown Rose, heard that authorities were after his father and took shortcuts to the Rose homestead in the Potts' Creek Valley by horseback. Jackson quickly sought support against the patrol, but the local Unionists decided against physical confrontation. Disgruntled, Rose swore to fight them by himself if he had to.[10]

The armed band arrived at Rose's house. The soldiers found Jackson's wife, Ruth Wolf Rose. Daughter Tabitha and her twin children were also present. Harvey was sitting quietly by the fireplace. The soldier inquired about Harvey's age, believing he might be of age to fight. Ruth lied, and due to Harvey's diminutive size, she was believed. In a search that followed, Jackson was found. A short fight followed during which Ruth received a bayonet wound. Jackson tried to injure one of the intruders with a homemade sword made of a cradle blade, but when the sword got caught in the ceiling rafters, Jackson had no chance to escape.[11]

---

[9] Gen. A.A. Chapman to C.S. Commissioner Sidney S. Baxter, Feb. 12, 1862, RG109, M437, roll 31, National Archives.

[10] Bostic Interview, April, 1988.

[11] Bostic Interview, April, 1988; Dorothy Cook Interview by phone, Jan. 1990; Report of Sydney S. Baxter, RG109, M437, roll 31, National Archives; James Bradley Interview, Paint Bank, VA, Jan. 1993.

The soldiers took Jackson away. His black hair was said to have been pulled out in hanks, and his blood covered the snow. Brought before General Chapman once again, Rose was not released. Rather, he went to Richmond under a heavy guard. His company captain, Gibbons Figgatt, traveled along as a witness. Chapman wrote to Confederate Provost General John Henry Winder in Richmond that Rose was a dangerous man, and suggested that he remain as a prisoner in Richmond. Commissioner Sidney S. Baxter agreed. Baxter stated Rose's trial was to be in Craig County. Rose and other civilian prisoners from western Virginia languished in Castle Thunder in Richmond. Rose remained in Richmond until about May 1862. That month, Rose signed a petition requesting permission to travel beyond the lines of the Federal Army in order to provide for his family. The plea went unnoticed. In mid-February, citizens of the Paint Bank area circulated a petition for leniency in Rose's behalf. The petition found its way to Baxter, who dismissed it summarily. Among the signatures were local citizens (and Unionists) Allen and Abe Armentrout, and Field A., Washington, and John E. Jarvis. [12]

Jackson Rose was not the only prisoner taken to Richmond that cold February. Other people arrested at

---

[12] Viola Martin Interview, Catawba, VA, Mar. 1989; Gen. A.A. Chapman to Provost Gen. John Henry Winder, Feb. 12, 1862, RG109, M437, Roll 31, National Archives; Petitions dated Feb. 18, 1862, RG109, M437, Roll 31, National Archives; Petition dated May 18, 1862, RG109, M437, Roll 33, National Archives.

the time were Jefferson I. Mann and Fielding Boggs of Greenbrier County. "VBF Boggs and made oath that in a conversation with Fielding Boggs on Sunday, the 26th day of Jan. 1862, he said that he was a Secessionist but in a conversation turned in favor of the Union and that the Malitia [sic] were all fools for going out to fight the North...."[13]

Some arrests led to clues of actual Unionists with their own solutions to impressment. A Hardy County resident named John Tucker was mentioned in several testimonial accounts in the region. Tucker was the leader of the "Swamp Guards," a group of armed Unionists. Most of the arrests were based on little more than hearsay since allegations, rumors, and conversation were enough to arrest a civilian suspected of disloyalty.[14] Paranoia had set in.

I send by Major Smith & others ten prisoners Viz Robert Atkins, David Bragg Henry Wiles John Atkins Adam Bragg, Mansen Kincaid Geo W Crook Thomas Sexton Jackson Rose and William Smith--they are what are documented Union men....the most dangerous men to our cause in the whole Country as they act as spys & guides to the enemy.[15]

[13] J.J. Wilken Affidavit, undated, RG109, M437, roll 31, National Archives.

[14] Report of S.S. Baxter, undated, subject--John Byar, RG109, M437, Roll 31, National Archives.

[15] Chapman to Winder, Feb. 12, 1862, RG109, M437, roll 31, National Archives.

Despite a huge effort to have them released, Rose and his friend William Smith bided their time in prison. On February 26, 1862, Colonel Rowan arrived in Richmond to assume a political vacancy. Rowan wrote that Rose may have duly influenced Smith. Rowan indicated that Smith should rejoin the Army. The political influence was enough to have Smith released. Rose was not that lucky.[16]

Rose's old unit and colleagues continued their protective watch. It was not without consequence. General Chapman's troops continued to march until spring. On March 24, Back Valley resident Allen Armentrout enlisted in Confederate Captain Lemons's Company. He became ill with what was thought to be malaria after a month of service. Armentrout simply fell out of the line of march and walked away. No one dared to stop him.[17]

Whether or not Armentrout actually had malaria, there was no doubt that April 1862 was a pivotal time of regional Union sentiment. Residents served in the militia or encountered frequent local patrols, but they rarely saw the effects of war in other personal fashions. Previously, no one had lawfully forced civilians to join the Confederate Army. Enlistment had been strongly encouraged or considered a duty for local defense. Afterward, local officials steadily lost control of the military affairs of the region to Richmond. The Conscription Act, did damage

---

[16] John Rowan to Baxter, Feb. 26, 1862, RG109, M437, Roll 31, National Archives.

[17] Allen Armentrout Service Record, Item 17, RG109, M324, Roll 1053, National Archives; Lafe Armentrout Interview by phone, April 1992.

to the Confederate cause in Monroe, Craig, and Alleghany Counties. The yeoman farmers had the most to lose. They had to sacrifice their sons or themselves to service in the Confederate Army. Some would gladly go, feeling service an honor. However, many in this mountainous region felt differently.

The Conscription Act hardened the opposition, and made the term "Unionist" difficult to define. A description of a Unionist prior to April 1862 had been a citizen who opposed secession or talked of a sustained Union. Following the effective date of the Act, the "Unionist" definition was extended to include conscription dodgers and pacifists. Most of the western Virginia Unionists were of the pacifist variety.

The Conscription Act required all eligible males to enlist, and, as a result, new regiments were forming or in the process of formation throughout this time. The 22nd Virginia Regiment added Craig boys to their ranks. General Chapman's son, George Beirne Chapman, formed his own company at Lewisburg and Union.[18]

One reason for all the activity was the action on the front lines. In early spring 1862, General George McClellan was the Commander-in-Chief of the Federal forces. The Confederate stronghold at Manassas had a force in that vicinity. Confederate General Joseph E. Johnston decided to find a more defensible line further south. Johnston kept McClellan guessing by painting logs with black paint and giving the Federals an impres-

---

[18] Lowry, 22nd Virginia Infantry, 103; J.L. Scott, Lowry's, Bryan's, and Chapman's Batteries , 71.

sion the Confederate forces were still there. These "Quaker guns," as they were called, gave the vital time necessary to drop back.[19]

In April, McClellan landed a large Federal force near Yorktown, Virginia. Given little choice, Johnston delayed McClellan's advance toward Richmond. Cautious as McClellan was, a siege near Yorktown detained the advance nearly a month. Johnston slowly dropped back toward Richmond.[20]

Robert E. Lee, at his Richmond headquarters, had good reason to worry. The initial wave of enthusiasm for a Southern Confederacy had receded, and jubilation became fear. The Manassas victory was ancient history. McClellan was at Richmond's door; volunteer enlistments declined; and the terms of many volunteers were ending. A part-time army would no longer hold the trenches.[21]

In western Virginia a revolt against the Conscription Act was forthcoming. In Alleghany County, along Potts' Creek, two of the Wolf boys were killed for resisting enlistment. The local patrols left one hanging dead on a fence. In Craig County, John J. Morgan refused to enlist. He was later shot dead in his own backyard. Field A. Jarvis' two nephews, George and James Linton,

---

[19] McPherson, Ordeal by Fire (New York: Alfred A. Knopf, 1982), 235 [permission given by McGraw-Hill].

[20] Ibid., 236-237.

[21] Tatum, Disloyalty in the Confederacy (Chapel Hill, NC: U. of North Carolina Press, 1934), 13-14.

sought shelter in the woods from the patrols. At night when safe, Field's daughter Matilda passed plates of food out a back kitchen window. Her brother Joseph was outside the window and took the food to the woods to feed the two hungry refugees. In an affidavit, Mary S. E. Linton and Euphemia N. Linton claimed to have carried provisions to Field, so that the Linton brothers could be fed at night. In a different claim, George A. Linton testified that food arrived at the Jarvis home. Field sometimes carried the food to the deserters' camps on Potts' Mountain. According to Linton, Field was trusted with the locations of the camps in the neighborhood.[22]

The camps existed due to the local recruiting activities of the 22nd Virginia Infantry. Almost all of these men enlisted at White Sulphur Springs, Greenbrier County, on May 1, 1862. One local, John L. Hellems, a wagoner, deserted on May 30, 1862.[23]

Deserters were soon a secondary problem to invading Union troops. On May 1, Confederates burned the town of Princeton in Mercer County when a fast advance by Federal troops of Colonel Rutherford B. Hayes threat-

---

[22] Thurmon Reynolds Interview, Covington, VA, July 1990; Lucy Hurst Interview, Roanoke, VA, Nov. 1992; Viola Martin Interview, Nov. 1989; Euphemia and Mary S.E. Linton Affidavit, Jan. 27, 1880, in Field A. Jarvis Pension, RG15, National Archives; George A. and William Linton Affidavit, Jan. 27, 1880, in Field A. Jarvis Pension, RG15, National Archives.

[23] Lowry, 22nd Virginia, 103; Ibid., 169.

ened to take supplies stored there. General Cox's men formally occupied the town on May 17.[24]

In Alleghany County, Federal Colonel George Crook raided. Crook suddenly turned back west, and his troops reached the town of Lewisburg. By May 12, the Union troops held the town. Confederates under General Henry Heth surprised the Federals on May 23rd. His disjointed attack soon fell apart. Crook's men forced the confused Confederates back across the Greenbrier River into Monroe. The Confederates burned the bridge behind them to prevent pursuit.[25]

The nearness of the Federal troops escalated the activities of all Unionists, pseudo-Unionists, or pacifists in the region. S.R. Houston noted in his diary, "Sherwood, a militiaman who refused to go into the service and tried to make his escape was shot through the knee today."[26] On May 5th, Houston wrote:

Some Union men stole three horses from farmers within nine miles of this village last Saturday. A suspected accomplice was brought to town yesterday. Eight men, 20 wagons full of provisions, and 90 horses taken near Wythville (?) a few days ago.[27]

The presence of Unionists, and the lack of Confederate presence, only made attitudes worse. Heth's Army

---

[24] Stan Cohen, The Civil War in West Virginia, 79.

[25] Ibid., 82; Morton, Monroe, 153.

[26] Morton, Monroe, S.R. Houston Diary, March 31, 1862, 173.

[27] Ibid., May 5, 1862, 174.

lodged at Salt Sulphur Springs after the battle. He left only an infantry company to guard Union. Local leaders about Union bristled with anger at the lull in security. A few days before, Confederate pickets at the river had been driven in.[28]

The Federals were too close, and local leaders had seen enough. Oliver Beirne and General Chapman wrote privately to George Wythe Randolph, the Confederate Secretary of War. They suggested Heth should be transferred elsewhere. The local leaders felt his every endeavor in the region had failed. Beirne and Chapman were particularly irate about Heth's initial retreat beyond Union after the Battle of Lewisburg. As a result, Federal raids in the county captured livestock and slaves.[29]

The Federal raids shifted attention away from the Unionists and to the threat just outside. This shift would be a turning point for the Unionists, who were encouraged by the presence of Union troops. Some managed to slip out behind the lines. Henry Tingler left his family behind and went through "rather than to swell their ranks."[30]

---

[28] Morton, Monroe, 151; A. A. Chapman and Oliver Beirne to Confederate Sec. of War George Wythe Randolph, July 3, 1862, OR, Series 1, Vol. 52, pt. 2, 326.

[29] Chapman and Beirne to Randolph, July 3, 1862, OR, Vol. 52, pt. 2, 326-327.

[30] George A. Linton Testimony, Question 57 in Henry Tingler, SCC File 5006, RG233, M1407, Fishe 3221, National Archives.

The result of the Beirne/Chapman letter was bureaucracy in motion. Randolph felt others in the region and beyond disagreed with their sentiments. Randolph was referring to career military men. Still, the letter was referred to Confederate President Jefferson Davis, who felt the criticism of Heth was unprofessional. The disregard for local leaders fed the fires of local Unionists. They were too happy to see the lack of cooperation between Richmond and local Confederates.[31]

The civilian approach did not work. So the local forces in Monroe County tried self-help. Local military organization in Monroe improved with the office of Monroe County's first wartime Provost Marshal, Allen Taylor Caperton. General Heth himself had recommended Caperton. By March 1862, the appointment became effective. For the remainder of the Civil War, Monroe was to be under martial constraints. Caperton would soon prove adept at the task.[32]

While Caperton improved the local morale, Heth was not so lucky. His unpopularity led to his removal from the region. Despite his favored status in Richmond from Confederate military leaders, Heth's own troops resented him. By the end of July, General Loring took over.[33]

---

[31] First and second endorsements on Beirne and Chapman letter to Randolph, July 3, 1862, OR, Vol. 52, pt. 2, 327.

[32] Morton, Monroe, 161.

[33] Brig. Gen. Henry Heth to Maj. Gen. William W. Loring, May 23, 1862, OR, Vol. 12, pt. 1, 812-813; Morton, Monroe, 153.

General William Wing Loring was a career military man. He had fallen out with "Stonewall" Jackson the previous winter. Most importantly, Loring was familiar with western Virginia and its people.[34]

Loring boosted Confederate morale by a grand review in a field near Union on July 26th. The line was over a mile-and-a-half long. Loring focused on the increasing problem of desertion. To restock his ranks and embarrass deserters, Loring published broadsides that listed the names of deserters by regiment. He also strengthened local ties. For example, Loring and his staff visited the Sweet Springs home of Oliver Beirne. Still, some maintained the cause of Loring's visits was not only to improve morale but to court the pretty daughter of Mr. Beirne. In any case, Loring greatly assisted local efforts to control their civilians.[35]

Loring's job was made easier by an active Caperton, but the Unionists were bolder. Deserters clung to the mountainous terrain, while police patrols enforced Loring's code. On the 30th of July, S.R. Houston noted in his diary:

---

[34] Cohen, Civil War in West Virginia, 77; Ibid., 85.

[35] Morton, Monroe, Houston Diary, July 26, 1862, 175; West Virginia University, Roy Bird Cook Collections, Broadsides for 22nd VA Infantry and 8th Virginia Cavalry; David L. Phillips, ed., War Stories: The Civil War in West Virginia, 321; Cohen, Civil War in West Virginia, 91.

We in some danger crossing Sweet Springs Mountain. Deserters very numerous there. While the police officers were bringing to the hotel three of them yesterday, they were fired upon by 16 others, and one deserter was killed by mistake.[36]

One of the more controversial cases of local conflict during this period was that of William Ballard of Rock Camp. Ballard left Confederate lines during the summer of 1862. His accusers stated he "went into the enimies [sic] camp, taking with him one of his sons a conscript in the Confederate States army and two or three other deserters all of whom are still with the enemy."[37]

Upon his return, Ballard was captured and sent to Richmond. That was the official story. Rumors persisted that he never reached prison alive. At a bridge, he was thrown into a creek by his captors. One of the soldiers yelled that a prisoner was trying to escape. Ballard was shot as he tried to get out of the water.[38]

Perhaps more embarrassing for local authorities was the scandal caused by local police after the confiscation of Ballard's property. His estate was sold that September.[39]

---

[36] Morton, Monroe, Houston Diary, July 30, 1862, 176.

[37] A. A. Chapman to Maj. Gen. Samuel Jones, Mar. 24, 1863, RG109, roll 98, National Archives; Ballard, William Ballard--A Genealogical Record, 28.

[38] Ballard, 28.

[39] A.A. Chapman to Maj. Gen. Samuel Jones, Mar. 24, 1863, RG109, M437, roll 98, National Archives.

To attempt to make disposition of the property of disloyal persons in the country where municipal law is abrogated & martial law instituted in its place, and to Audit the claims of loyals persons on the same by military investigation & action would be too onerous a task on the Commds General and would produce results of very doubtful justice and equity to the persons interested....It strikes me as a better course than to resort to the perplexity of a military Administration on such estates, that the President be asked to revivie the jurisdiction of the Confederate Court in the Western District of Virginia, where the same is suspended by the proclamation of martial laws....[40]

With the reluctance of the Confederate Army to be involved, Caperton sold Ballard's estate, bringing in a total of $892.53. The sale's bad reputation would pester local leaders for the next year. It hardened Unionist resistance, which could play upon Ballard as a martyred man.[41]

The worries were for nothing. Soon, Loring went westward and into the Kanawha Valley. His troops fought Federals at Fayetteville and up the Kanawha River

---

[40] Chief of Staff Henry Fitzhugh to Allen T. Caperton, Aug. 27, 1862, RG109, M437, roll 98, National Archives.

[41] A. A. Chapman Report to Maj. Gen. Jones, March 24, 1863, J111-1863, RG109, M437, roll 98, National Archives.

towards Charleston. The Federals, under General Andrew Jackson Lightburn, steadily retreated. By Mid-September, Charleston fell and Lightburn fled toward the Ohio River. The victory did not last. The Federals landed troops near Point Pleasant and prepared to retake the city. Knowing he could not hold out against a larger force, Loring abandoned Charleston. He dropped back without orders. For this error, Loring was replaced by General John Echols.[42]

In some respects, it was a mistake to replace Loring. Unionists and Union soldiers were at a psychological disadvantage. A swift movement could have retaken some of the lost ground. Loring's ability to improve morale was vital in the region. Neither Heth nor Echols instilled such effect.

Echols had one advantage. He was local. Echols received respect in Richmond and bridged the gap between local and general Confederate goals in the region.

Whoever the local leader, it made little difference to local civilians already arrested. Jackson Rose was jailed at Salisbury, North Carolina, to where many western Virginia civilians had been removed. North Carolina's politicians viewed the prison as a dismal place.[43]

> To overawe the struggling Union sentiment
> of our people, the one at Salisbury [North
> Carolina] was set up and made the scence

---

[42] Cohen, <u>Civil War in West Virginia</u>, 85-86.

[43] Louis Brown, <u>The Salisbury Prison--A Case Study of Confederate Military Prisons 1861-1865</u> (Wendell, NC: Avera Press, 1980), 62-63; Bostic Interview, Aug. 1988.

[sic] of horrors, at the recollection of which the blood still runs cold. Hundreds of our private citizens, exempt from conscription, were there....[44]

The history of Salisbury was as dismal as its description. By early 1862, civilian prisoners from western Virginia were first mentioned in Salisbury. On June 21, some citizen prisoners plotted to escape. The plot failed. The following month, another failed effort took place. By the autumn of 1863, 50 civilians from east Tennessee and western Virginia were there.[45]

Other period lists revealed the local western Virginian's presence in Confederate custody. A list of 262 citizen prisoners was submitted by Confederate Commissioner Robert Ould. The list named those confined at Castle Thunder (called Eastern District Station) up to February 12, 1863. Among those listed from Monroe County were an unnamed Ballard (probably Lewis), Nicholas Martin, and Jackson Rose.[46]

Some time after May 1862, Rose came to Salisbury. The squalid conditions promoted disease. Jackson

---

[44] William C. Harris, "Southern Unionist Critique of the Civil War," Civil War History--A Journal of the Middle Period, March 1985, No. 1, Kent State University Press, John T. Hubbell, ed., 53.

[45] Brown, Salisbury Prison, 63-64.

[46] Citizen Prisoners Eastern District Station, Feb. 12, 1863, RG249, Roll 691, Miscellaneous Rolls of Federal Prisoners 1861-65, National Archives.

caught dropsy and died in December. A friend asked Rose if he had any message for his family. Jackson replied that he did not. Rose believed his family perished. In fact, three of his sons crossed the Ohio River into Gallia County, Ohio.[47]

At almost the same time, the first of many supply shortages became apparent. By November 1, wagons attempting to bring back salt for the Confederacy turned back in the Kanawha Valley. The Federals had returned. They occupied almost the very same positions they had the previous winter. The season was harsh for the civilians, who were lacking food and provisions. S.R. Houston wrote, "It is thought a famine is threatening us."[48]

---

[47] Jackson Rose Death Record, West Virginia Vital Statistics, Virginia State Archives, filmed by the Genealogical Society of Utah, 1954, 62D; Thurman Reynolds Interview, Covington, VA, July 1990; Bostic Interview, Dec. 1989.

[48] Morton, Monroe, Houston Diary, Nov. 1, 1862, 176; Ibid., Nov. 22, 1862, 176.

CHAPTER THREE

HORSE AND SABER--1863

In many ways, 1863 characterized the best and worst of the war. The year 1863 was the year of Gettysburg, Chancellorsville, and Chickamauga Creek. In western Virginia, the battles fought were White Sulphur Springs, Droop Mountain, and Averell's Salem Raid. There was a regional lull in war activity from November 1862 until August 1863. Provisions became the most important concern. Major campaigns were elsewhere.

The lull could be interpreted in three ways. The first was exhaustion of the armies. The year 1863 taxed the resources and manpower of both sides. It would take time for the Federals to consolidate their forces. Confederate offensive and defensive maneuvers later that year left troops threadbare and ready for rest.

The second explanation for a lull was geographical. Western Virginia proved too difficult a terrain for Federals to launch a major offensive. The bad roads, craggy mountains, and deep waters just made the effort unproductive. Lincoln and his generals looked elsewhere for an easier victory. In the region, the Federals were fighting a defensive war. They fended off more Confederate advances than they themselves advanced.

The last possible reason for regional inactivity was Confederate strategy. General Lee's Army of Northern

Virginia was across the Rappahannock River from the Federals. Too many other towns and cities had to be defended before allowing any major campaign in western Virginia.

Whatever the ultimate reason, only a series of small raids took place until August 1863, when raids occurred on a larger scale. A period of retrenchment took place. Periodically, each side would prod the other with light infantry or cavalry.

This kind of probe took place at Fayetteville in May 1863 and in the Jones-Imboden Raid that April and May. The Confederates launched most of their offensive probes the first half of the year. The Federal raids dominated the second half.

The most notable Confederate effort in the early spring of 1863 was William L. "Mudwall" Jackson's expedition to Beverly, Virginia. However, Jackson gathered a sizeable number of troops to surround the town. Once Jackson lost his surprise initiative, he abandoned his efforts.[1]

These efforts were little more than an annoyance to the Federals. Neither side was truly strong enough to fully overrun the other's position. For that same reason, local Unionists could not be deterred from their activity.

A good example of Unionist activity during this period involved a group of bushwhackers that tried to assassinate "Mudwall" Jackson. A little girl carried some

---

[1] Cohen, Civil War in West Virginia, 93-94; A.S. Johnston, Captain Beirne Chapman and Chapman's Battery, (Union, WV: Monroe Watchman by permission of the Johnston Family, 1991), 12-13.

flowers to Jackson as he passed. This was used as a signal to fire upon the General since few of the Unionist bushwhackers in Pocohontas County knew what Jackson looked like. Guns fired, but Jackson escaped unscathed. After detaining the little girl for a time, she obtained her freedom.[2]

There was great significance to Jackson's narrow escape. Although it did not take place in Monroe, Craig, or Greenbrier Counties, the attack took place in a county similar to the three and within close proximity. The difference was aggressive Unionists. The bushwhackers progressed to physical violence upon a major Confederate military figures, such as Jackson.

The Monroe area Unionists would remain in a defensive role. However, bushwhacking was no longer considered a defensive tactic. The bushwhacker's organization in the regions was so sporadic that little use had come of it. Therefore, Monroe Unionists could not be considered an effective entity to fight the Confederate soldiers and local police units.

From early 1863, the Unionists became more aggressive in their tactics and much more organized. A secret society, the Loyal Order of the Heroes of America, was started by several North Carolinians. The Heroes of America worked its way north and west, mostly recruiting mountain farmers along the Appalachian chain. The actual founder was a man named John Pool, who spent some time imprisoned in Richmond. Pool traveled through western Virginia in 1864. The Heroes of America were sometimes called the "Red String" because

---

[2] Johnston, <u>Chapman's Battery</u>, 13.

of a colored thread members would wear in the lapel of their coats as a signal to one another. Interestingly, Henderson Adams, North Carolina's State Auditor, was a founding member of the Order.[3]

The arrival of the Heroes of America forced a change in the goals of the Federal leadership. There were no heavy forces under General Cox or Rosecrans. Federal Generals Elichim Scammon and William Woods Averell were the leading military leaders. Averell would make a lasting impact within the coming months.[4]

Averell was hitherto luckless. He did not fare well in cavalry battles at Kelly's Ford, Virginia, against Confederate General James Ewell Brown (JEB) Stuart. As a result, Averell became a political scapegoat. He went westward, like so many other less fortunate generals. Only one thing separated Averell from those other generals. Averell wished to be back in the main theatre of operations. He intended to succeed in his operations in western Virginia.[5]

While Averell was making plans, the Confederate leaders in Monroe started to feel the financial burden of military occupation. The spring of 1863 found Confederate General John S. Williams at Salt Sulphur Springs, where he boarded at $8.00 a month with his staff. By the 9th of April, Williams owed $338.00 for the boarding of

[3] Tatum, Disloyalty in the Confederacy, 158; Charles H. Wesley, Collapse of the Confederacy (Washington, D.C.: The Associated Publishers, Inc., 1937), 95.

[4] Cohen, Civil War in West Virginia, 103.

[5] Robert B. Boehm, "The Unfortunate Averell," Civil War Times Illustrated, Vol. V, No. 5, Aug. 1966, 32.

his staff since January 1, 1863. Although William Erskine did his best to collect it, he died early in 1863.[6]

Personal finances and fortunes also affected the common soldier. Alexander C. Looney sent a petition to the Confederate authorities near the Back Valley to Richmond in January to have himself removed from active service in the 22nd Virginia Infantry. Looney asked to be detailed as a tanner, as "his father, Moses Looney, being old and feeble health, and having on hand a good lot of hides" needed him. Some of the signatures on Looney's petition were Isaac R. Wolf, John Goode, Adam Myers, and Thomas N. Been. Goode and Wolf were Unionists too old to face conscription.[7]

Perhaps to help alleviate the impending financial burden, Confederate General Samuel Jones issued an order to sell the property of Unionists who had previously fled the region. Colonel Wilson Lively of the Monroe County Police carried out the sale of property belonging to the Kesinger, Smith, and Ellison families. The properties were sold per Jones' order of January 31st.[8]

---

[6] Form no. 22, Apr. 22, 1863, Confederate Papers Relating to Citizens or Business Firms, RG109, M346, Roll 286, National Archives, Washington, D.C.

[7] Petition for Alexander Looney, Jan. 21, 1863, RG109, M437, roll 100, National Archives, Washington, D.C.

[8] A.A. Chapman to Maj. Gen. Samuel Jones, Mar. 24, 1863, RG109, M437, Roll 98, National Archives; N. Harrison to Confederate Sec. of War James A. Seddon, July 24, 1863, RG109, M474, Roll 61, National Archives, Washington, D.C.

51

Beverly Ballard of Greenville was arrested January 1st near Salt Sulphur, and brought before General Williams. Naturally, his sentiments drew suspicion. Ballard's neighbor, Matthew Campbell, asked him to assist in the blockade of a road from Salt Sulphur to Peter's Mountain. Ballard declined, and Campbell, feeling this a disloyal act, threatened him. As there was little evidence to hold Ballard on, he was set free the next day. Ballard's residence, only four miles from Union, made him a likely target due to the proximity of local Confederate authorities. He soon removed to a farm near Dropping Lick, some miles distant.[9]

Also some distance from Union, and in some danger, was John Goode. The Craig County resident was known as a Unionist, despite the fact that several of Goode's sons were in the Confederate Army. His sister, Mary Jane, was married to a Craig County school teacher, James Reynolds. It was Reynolds' son-in-law, John J. Morgan, who was killed the previous year for defying the Conscription Act. Goode was also a friend of John Webb, one of the first arrested for his sentiments in the region. Goode was categorized as one of several ex-Whig slaveholders that obeyed Lincoln's Emancipation Proclamation. Goode also had a prosperous farm located in a prime spot along Craig's Creek.[10]

---

[9] Questions 24 and 26, Beverly Ballard SCC claim, no. 16145, RG233, M1407, fishe 1838, National Archives, Washington, D.C.

[10] Question 30, John Goode Testimony, Sept. 9, 1872, in John Goode SCC claim, RG123, National Archives; Ibid., Question 40; Bostic Interview, Oct. 1988; Lucy B.

continued on next page

The next place below the Spessard place is the Goode place. Old man Billy Goode lived in the house below the road, opposite and slightly below the Bal Carper House....Old man Johnny Goode lived in a house further out in the field....old man Johnny Goode had a blacksmith shop on the opposite side of the road from Mountain View Church....[11]

The location was not a blessing. Goode's farm would see much more of the war. Later, war appeared on his very doorstep.[12]

Other local Unionists went to the war instead of the reverse. Allen B. Wiley had a different story. He grew up near what became Paint Bank and slipped through the lines once the Campaign of 1861 was finished. Allen was the youngest of the four sons of James and Sarah Wiley. Because of neighborhood sentiment, there was no surprise that Wiley went to Ohio to join Company D, 47th Ohio Infantry. He headed west with his regiment to Louisville, Memphis, and finally Vicksburg. In the latter campaign, Wiley fell ill. Sent to St. Louis by passenger boat, Wiley wrote to his brother.[13]

Hurst Interview, Nov. 1992; Mabel Lee Damewood, About Craig Valley (New Castle, VA: Craig Co. Historical Society, n.d.), 14; James Reynolds Family, Craig County, Eighth Census, RG29, M653, Roll 1341, National Archives, Washington, D.C.

[11] Damewood, About Craig Valley, 14.

[12] John Goode Testimony, Sept. 9, 1872, in John Goode SCC claim, RG123, National Archives.

[13] General Affadavit, Sarah Wiley, Dec. 30, 1879, in Sarah Wiley pension 238394, RG15, National Archives,

continued on next page

I am very low at present but I hope you are enjoying good heth [sic] Dear Brother I has been sick ever sinse [sic] saw you last and I am scarsly abil [sic] to walk I have something like brest [sic] complaint I have fell away 50 pounds.[14]

Allen B. Wiley died of phthisis on April 9th, 1863. In his last letter, Wiley wished everyone well, knowing he was going to die. The word soon reached Wiley's old neighborhood, and the reaction would only fuel future Unionist efforts. Loyal Confederate citizenry were not thinking much of the Unionists.[15]

Manpower was not the only commodity in short supply. Alleghany County resident William C. Clark was asked to purchase cotton yarn, but because of a shortage, he was only able to purchase a portion of the cloth needed.[16]

Cotton was not the only commodity in short supply. Many natural resources could not be easily obtained. Salt was in great shortage. Saltpeter, used to make gunpowder, was also hard to come by. One of the region's greatest losses, however, came in manual labor. Above the sons taken to fight, 27 of Alleghany's 225

Washington, D.C.; A.B. Wiley to unnamed brother, Feb. 4, 1863, in Sarah Wiley pension, RG15, National Archives.

[14] A.B. Wiley to unnamed brother, Feb. 4, 1863, in Sarah Wiley pension, RG15, National Archives.

[15] Ibid.

[16] Morton, Alleghany, 54.

slaves worked directly under the Confederate Government.[17]

As the Civil War continued, the Confederacy used its military capability to control the expression of sentiment in local populations. The Confederate/local government cooperation grew stronger. Confederate troops did not interfere, when asked not to, with the local jurisdictions.

> Lt. Saunders has been instructed not to interfere with the police guard of Monroe Co. His especial business is to attend to the collecting of conscripts and deserters in Mercer and Raleigh. He thinks that the property of men who have deserted to the enemy should be taken possession of by the receiver under the Confiscative or Sequestration act [sic]....[18]

Cooperation did not always exist from the Confederate high command. Confederate Secretary of War James Seddon heard of the William Ballard property sale. General Samuel Jones was obliged to report to Seddon on the specific circumstances of Ballard's capture. Jones' reaction was to distance himself. He stated he was absent during most of the events that surrounded Ballard's death. Augustus Chapman, who in January, 1863, had

---

[17] Ibid.

[18] W.B. Myers to General A.A. Chapman, Jan. 30, 1863, RG109, M474, roll 61, National Archives, Washington, D.C.

become the new Provost Marshal in Union, likewise distanced himself.[19]

Col. Wilson Lively a member of House of Delegates of Virginia from this county--and the Assistant Pro. Marshal for the lower end of the County--has just arrived here and I am enabled from his report to make satisfactory answers to most of the interrogatives propounded by the War Department in regard to the sale of the property of William Ballard Decd....[20]

Chapman's response was to affirm that the confiscated Ballard property was taken with the approval of Generals Heth and Loring. The incident had taken place in the term of the previous Provost Marshal. Seddon frowned on the distribution of a deserter's property while the area was under general martial law. Therefore, Richmond felt the affair was above the county jurisdiction.[21]

Locally, 1863 would be John Echols' year. While the previous year's Confederate regional command was split between the tainted personalities of Heth and Lor-

[19] Gen. Samuel Jones to Confederate Secretary of War James A. Seddon, Mar. 31, 1863, RG109, M437, roll 98, National Archives; Morton, Monroe, 162; A.A. Chapman to Gen. Samuel Jones, Mar. 24, 1863, RG109, M437, Roll 98, National Archives.

[20] Attachment C, A.A. Chapman to Jones, Mar. 24, 1863, RG109, M437, Roll 98, National Archives, Washington, D.C.

[21] Ibid.; Jones to Seddon, Mar. 31, 1863, RG109, M437, Roll 98, National Archives, Washington, D.C.

ing, Echols enjoyed great local popularity. General Sam Jones was the overall Department Commander of Confederate forces in the region. There was no doubt, however, that General John Echols was the spiritual leader of the soldiers. The year 1863 would be the height of Echols' military career. Jones was absent for long periods of time, often in East Tennessee, and Echols was left in charge locally. Echols never enjoyed good health and, consequently, would prove a better administrator than a field commander.[22]

Despite the new command in western Virginia, the war raged on in the east. In the spring, General Lee engaged the Federals at the Battle of Chancellorsville. The death of "Stonewall" Jackson was the cost of the Confederate victory. The war moved north. By mid-summer 1863, Lee's men fought decisively with the Federals at Gettysburg, Pennsylvania.

Many area troops from Craig County, fought at Gettysburg. John Landon Reynolds, James Reynolds' son, fell wounded in the thigh at Pickett's Charge. The losses at Gettysburg drained manpower both regionally and for the Confederacy in general.[23]

The battle lines moved elsewhere. After Gettysburg, war returned to Virginia. The Federals soon con-

---

[22] William C. Davis, The Battle of New Market (Baton Rouge, LA: Louisiana State U. Press, 1975), 39-40; Jones' command chart, OR, Series I, Vol. 29, Part 2, 812.

[23] Application for Disability by Wound, Jan. 4, 1908, Form No. 1, Act of 1902, in John Landon Reynolds Pension, filmed by Genealogical Society of Utah, 1990, Roll 86, Virginia State Archives, Richmond, VA.

solidated their forces in western Virginia. By late August, it was clear something would happen. S.R. Houston perhaps put it best in his diary entry for August 25, 1863: "Dispatch from General Jones to remove their effects out of the way, as a raid may be expected at any moment."[24]

The warning from Jones was no false alarm. Union General William Woods Averell, leading a large force of cavalry, raided much of the saltpeter works in the Alleghany County region. Averell's men rode as far as Callaghans, a short distance from the Alleghany County seat at Covington. The Confederates went after Averell in force, but the Federals rode back west toward the resort of Sweet Springs. Later, Averell turned north, toward White Sulphur Springs. Soon, Averell decided to raid Lewisburg, which had the law library of the Court of Appeals.[25]

Averell faced no easy task. Colonel George S. Patton of the 22nd Virginia commanded a combined force of Confederates that effectively blocked the road to Lewisburg. On the 26th, Averell gave battle. After some hours of stalemate, likely due to superior Confederate artillery, Averell retreated the next day.[26]

Near the Paint Bank region, Jane Jarvis Bostic and her newborn son, Marion Columbus Bostic, sat on top of a cave that contained their spring water and listened to

---

[24] Morton, History of Monroe, Houston Diary, Aug. 25, 1863, 177.

[25] Morton, Monroe, 153-154.

[26] Morton, Monroe, 153-154; Cohen, Civil War in West Virginia, 99.

58

the cannon fire in the distance. Somewhere in that battle was her husband, Private James A. Bostic, with Chapman's Battery. To the Jarvis Family, the war was getting too close to home.[27]

Unionists were thinking likewise. The Battle of White Sulphur Springs brought back the Confederate paranoia of late 1861 and early 1862. Military influence tightened the security of the local police. Augustus Chapman, as Provost Marshal, was replaced by Lieutenant Lysander S. Campbell of the 23rd Virginia Infantry about that very time. The Unionists needed to unite to defend themselves against a highly organized police presence. Campbell was not the only county-level appointee to have been a military figure. In Alleghany County, Confederate Lieutenant Herbert Dunn was the new Provost Marshal.[28]

Alleghany County instituted a Committee of Safety, which gathered in August. The panel was comprised of Peter Byers, William F. Clark, William Damron, Joseph Irvin, Thompson McAllister, and Charlton Shirkey. The formation of the Committee of Safety in Alleghany was the direct result of the Battle of White Sulphur Springs. Averell only turned back temporarily, but a mixture of caution and relief had spread over the people loyal to the Confederacy. S.R. Houston noted in

---

[27] Bostic Interview, Apr. 1988.

[28] Assistant Adjutant Gen. Charles Stringfellow to Inspector H.L. Clay, June 28, 1863, RG109, M474, Roll 61, National Archives.

his diary, "Our village was greatly relieved at the result of Dry Creek battle."[29]

After the battle, the Confederate Army camped nearby. The Federal drive stalled, but caution remained. Reverend Houston remarked many principal people of the county were not even attending church in Union. In time, they realized that there was good reason to fear.[30]

Most fighting in other war theatres ceased in the winter. Averell took his cavalry and light artillery and set out from Beverly. Averell's mission was simple. He was to disable or destroy the Virginia and Tennessee Railroad so that it was not usable for Confederate military use. The result could cut off reinforcements sent to Tennessee and the west. The Virginia and Tennessee Railroad was the main link between the two theatres and, if destroyed, could sever the two. While the mission was simple, the means were not.[31]

General Echols stood in the way of Averell's mission. Echols controlled the Greenbrier Valley after Averell retreated in August. Averell's movement was detected, and Echols occupied Droop Mountain in Pocohontas County. The Confederates held the high ground. On November 6, Averell's men found a weak point in

---

[29] Morton, Alleghany, 54; Morton, Monroe, Houston Diary, Aug. 27, 1863, 177.

[30] Morton, Monroe, Houston Diary, Sept. 6, 1863, 177.

[31] Cohen, Civil War in West Virginia, 102-103; Boehm, "The Unfortunate Averell," Civil War Times Illustrated, 33.

Echols line. The Federals rolled up a flank and sent the Confederates into a retreat.[32]

U.S. Brigadier General Alfred Duffie attempted to head off the Confederates before they reached Lewisburg but failed. Echols kept retreating until reaching Sinking Creek in Giles County. Averell was still short of his objective. The original goal to destroy the Virginia and Tennessee Railroad would be a priority until May 1864.[33]

Droop Mountain was a clear victory to the regional Unionists. The local police, while still performing their duties of seeking out local Union sympathizers, now had greater concerns. The Greenbrier Valley, although captured, proved to be temporary. The Federals soon withdrew back North, and the Confederates regained the region. However, the back of resistance broke. There was little to hold Averell back the next time.[34]

It would not be long to wait. In early December, Averell took his forces and headed southward. Many of the men Averell took with him were hardened veterans. Some of them were familiar with the vicinity. After departing from Keyser, West Virginia, Averell's men rode into Highland County. From there, he led his men southward into Craig County. Turning east along the Sweet Springs and Kanawha Turnpike, Averell's men rode past Sweet Springs. Taking advantage of fresh provisions, Averell's men confiscated whatever property

---

[32] Cohen, Civil War in West Virginia, 102.

[33] Boehm, "The Unfortunate Averell," 33; Johnston, Captain Beirne Chapman and Chapman's Battery, 15.

[34] Cohen, The Civil War in West Virginia, 102.

they thought appropriate. To his benefit, Averell knew of the existence of some Unionists in the region. Averell actively sought these people out to guide him or warn him of Confederate movements.[35]

As Averell's men passed, Jane Jarvis Bostic ran to a bell near her home and signaled an alarm to friends and family. Friend or foe did not matter at that moment. Their food and livestock were on the verge of seizure.[36]

Averell's goal was actually the town of Salem since the Virginia and Tennessee Railroad lay nearby. Along the way the Federals passed Widow Scott's Tavern on Middle Mountain. Some of Averell's men took notice of the farm of William Paxton, which was directly above the tavern. A few dismounted cavalrymen searched Paxton's farmhouse looking for food while the main entourage rested on the Turnpike. Surprising Paxton's pregnant wife, one of the soldiers pointed his pistol at her. The woman died of fright; however, this did not stop the soldiers from stealing provisions from the Paxton family.[37]

Ironically, William Paxton was a Unionist. A 51-year-old Campbellite Baptist and self-admitted Democrat, William "Billy" Paxton was not even present at his home when the soldiers came. Very shortly after the incident,

---

[35] Ibid., 103; William Paxton Testimony, Sept., 1872, in William Paxton SCC claim, RG123, National Archives, Washington, D.C.

[36] Bostic Interview, Aug. 1988.

[37] Cohen, The Civil War in West Virginia, 103; Question 2 & 13, William Paxton testimony, in William Paxton SCC claim, RG123, National Archives, Washington, D.C.

the horsed Paxton was captured by the pickets on the Turnpike. He was returning from the town of Fincastle, in Botetourt County, with his medication. The pickets took him to Scott's Tavern, where he was brought before General Averell himself.[38]

Paxton swore that he was a Unionist to Averell. By a stroke of luck, Paxton produced a letter written by four Union officers the previous summer. The letter, stated in whole, said:

Middle Mount, Craig Co., Va.

To all officers and soldiers of the U.S. Army; near Scott's farm, West Va., June 8

We the following commissioned officers of the U.S. Army, hereby certify that when within four miles of this place we were informed of the loyalty of Mr. Wm. Paxton and family, and forthwith we hastened to them. And we have found them in every way exhibiting evidence of extreme loyalty. They have fed us and entertained us and given us information and done many little things which can only be appreciated by persons who have been for weeks been leading a bushwhacking life.

---

[38] Question 10, William Paxton testimony, in William Paxton SCC Claim, Sept. 1872, RG123, National Archives, Washington, D.C.; Adam Myers testimony, in William Paxton SCC claim, Sept. 10, 1872; Lucy B. Hurst Family Group Sheets, Roanoke, VA.

We earnestly hope and sincerely trust
that all our forces will return their kindness
in every manner in their power.
Edmon Brice,
Lieut. Col. 19th Mass.
Delor Philips,
Capt. 17th Div. Vol. Infty.
Benjamin D. Saffore (or Laffore)
Lieut. 17th Mich. Vol. Infty.
Harrison Berden
2nd Lieut. 5th Mich. Cav.[39]

William Paxton was a Unionist, and, although
threatened with arrest, his condition and age kept him out
of Castle Thunder. Averell learned of the certificate and
accepted it to be genuine. However, there was a price
for freedom. Averell retained him as a guide until his
army reached Salem. Upon reaching the town, Averell
ordered Paxton and his horse released.[40]

At Salem, Averell's men tore up some track of the
railroad and burned a few buildings. Averell also knew
that the Confederates would not be slow in locating him,
so he again headed north. Heavy rains had swollen his
escape route across Craig's Creek, and the stream became too dangerous for the Federals to cross. Between

---

[39] Detached letter from four Union officers, June 8,
1863, in William Paxton SCC claim, RG123, National
Archives, Washington, D.C. Billy Paxton had true
possession of this letter. Oddly enough, he was never
seriously detained despite his assistance.

[40] Question 10, William Paxton testimony, in William
Paxton SCC Claim, Sept. 1872, RG123, National
Archives, Washington, D.C.; Ibid., Question 24.

William Paxton. Courtesy of Lucy B. Hurst

the 15th and 21st of December, Averell's men camped on the farm of John Goode. The Unionist Goode sent out his son William, a Confederate soldier in the 28th Virginia who was home on furlough, to tell the Federals of Confederate movements in the area. William Goode used the opportunity to flee.[41]

The occupation of the John Goode farm was not a kindly matter. Goode's fields were trampled by men and horses, and witness Edward Hancock claimed the men used Goode's fencing for firewood and freely ate the farm livestock as if it were their own. Craig's Creek was crossed as soon as possible, and Averell's men hurried on to avoid the Confederates.[42]

Once Averell approached Craig Court House, he knew that the Confederates had time enough to have gathered strength. Following the main thoroughfare of the James River Turnpike was certain disaster. Confederate General Echols waited on top of Sweet Springs Mountain. Soon, General Jones joined him. Colonel Jackson waited at Covington, and General Fitzhugh Lee's cavalry rode in from Staunton. The situation looked bleak for Averell. S.R. Houston noted in his diary, "Echols sent a dispatch stating the enemy would probably

---

[41] Cohen, Civil War in West Virginia, 103; Page 4, John Goode testimony, Sept. 9, 1872, in John Goode SCC claim, RG123, National Archives, Washington, D.C.; Ibid., Question 1; Frank Fields, 28th Virginia Infantry (Lynchburg, VA: H.E. Howard, 1985), 61.

[42] Question 1, Edward Hancock testimony, Sept. 18, 1872, in John Goode SCC claim, RG123, National Archives, Washington, D.C.

cross the mountain [Sweet Springs] on their return from Salem and be in the midst of us immediately."[43]

The only way Averell could escape was to find a guide. He settled on a doctor named Wylie. Averell gave the man and his family a choice of money or death. Whatever his sympathies may have been, Wylie had little choice. Averell did not have the time to argue about the issue, and a fast decision was made to remove Wylie's family to Union lines. Once word had gotten out of the doctor's aid to the Federals, even under duress, punishment was certain.[44]

Despite local aid, the Confederates were confident they would intercept Averell. Echols and Jones waited in vain. Wylie led the Union columns down a wagon road through the Rich Patch Valley in Alleghany County. The Federals passed the Jesse Humphries farm and Madison Hook's Hotel. The Rich Patch was an island of hope for the desperate Federals. It seemed to have a lot of the Unionist element: the Wolfs, Fridleys, Kings, Humphries, and Stulls.[45]

---

[43] Captain Benjamin White to Col. William L. Jackson, Dec. 19, 1863, OR, Vol. 29, pt 1, 965; Johnston, Captain Beirne Chapman and Chapman's Battery, 15-17; Morton, Monroe, Houston Diary, Dec. 19, 1863, 178.

[44] Johnston, Captain Beirne Chapman and Chapman's Battery, 17-18.

[45] Johnston, Captain Beirne Chapman and Chapman's Battery, 16; Louise C. Perkins, "Some Residents Supported the North", Virginian Review, June 6, 1989 (Covington, VA: Horton P. Beirne, pub.); White to Jackson, Dec. 19, 1863, OR, Vol. 29, pt. 1, 965.

continued on next page

Pressing on, Averell eluded capture by storming the Island Ford Bridge near Covington. Jackson's cavalry and a small contingent of home guard troops held the vulnerable spot. By the time Jones and Echols found out which direction Averell was headed and had sent men scrambling towards Callaghans, it was too late. The home guard troops ordered to burn the bridge started late, and Averell was able to save the structure. When the other Confederate commanders saw the smoke pillars near Covington, they realized that Averell had escaped.[46]

The embarrassment of Averell's successful escape was obvious. Someone had to take the blame. Colonel Jackson blamed a cavalry officer, William Arnett, for not blunting Averell's advance near Madison Hook's Hotel. Most blamed General Jones and called for his reassignment. Still others blamed Doctor Wylie and other Unionists for aiding and feeding the Federals. Realistically, all of these were to blame.[47]

Incidentally, the SCC claim of Jesse Humphries, Samuel Williams testimony of July 26, 1875, question 60, stated that the Humphries' farm was known as "Lincolnville." Jesse's wife, Eunice, had at least one brother, Roland Simmons, in the Union Army. Roland later settled in Kentucky.

[46] Johnston, Captain Beirne Chapman and Chapman's Battery, 16; Report of Col. William W. Arnett, 20th VA Cavalry, Dec. 29, 1863, OR, Vol. 29, part 1, 967-969.

[47] Captain John S. Spriggs to Col. William Jackson, Dec. 19, 1863, OR, Chap. 29, 965; Col. William L. Jackson to AAG Capt. R.H. Catlett, Dec. 28, 1863, OR, Vol. 29, pt. 1, 953-954; Johnston, Captain Beirne Chapman and Chapman's Battery, 16.

The primary reason for the successful raid was that the Confederates had underestimated Averell. Local leaders also realized they miscalculated the loyalties of their own citizens. Wylie was publicized as a traitor. There were more visible signs of Unionism, or at least pacifism and self-preservation, to give that appearance. As a result of the stigma, General Echols started trying to actually ferret out the disloyal citizens. One method Echols used was to send phony Federals among the populace to find the sources of trouble to them.[48]

Another reason for the escape was the sources of intelligence available to Averell. The soldiers he had with him were familiar with the terrain. They were not green, inexperienced men, and many of these had lived or had family in Monroe. Among such men were David R. Noble (Co. G and A, 7th WV Cavalry) and William G. Ballard (Co. H, 7th WV Cavalry).[49]

There was more than military campaigns in 1863. There was a trend forming. The trend took the form of petty jealousies, finger pointing, and the pain of losing a

---

[48] Johnston, Captain Beirne Chapman and Chapman's Battery, 16; Newlin, A Story of the War--Hitherto Unrecorded--An Account of the Escape of Six Federal Soldiers (Cincinnati, OH: Western Methodist Book Concern, 1870), 91-92; Seddon to Davis, Nov. 8, 1864, OR, Series IV, Vol. 3, 803; Enclosure, Robert L. Custin and James P. Hammet to Major, Aug. 28, 1864, 805.

[49] Service Record for Wm. Ballard, Item 164, RG94, Compiled Service Records of Volunteer Union Soldiers who Served in Organizations from West Virginia, M508, Roll 69, National Archives, Washington, D.C.; Ibid., David R. Noble, item 1646, Roll 72.

family member or a friend to a bullet. Families in the Paint Bank area experienced the hardships of family separation in 1863.

> Dir. to Ruth Rose for fournishing [sic] a hand and getting fire wood for Fleming Travors [sic] family seven days at one dollar a day--Also cutting and halling [sic] fire wood for James Roses family five days at 1.50 per day....7.50 not allowed by committee....[50]

Ruth Wolf Rose was a widow and then forced to be a provider. She hauled firewood for her son-in-law, Fleming Trenor, a soldier in the 60th Virginia Infantry. Such was the plight of many families in the area.[51]

At Droop Mountain, Mason V. Hellems, a soldier in the 22nd Virginia and a resident of the Back Valley area, fell mortally wounded. An officer in his unit sadly wrote,

> After awhile an ambulance came up. Another man was put in, I recognized the other man. It was poor Mason Helms of my company. He had been shot through the head and the body and had a finger shot off. He

---

[50] Loose Papers, Civil War File, Monroe County Courthouse, Union, WV. The Civil War File at the Courthouse was assembled in the 1940's or 1950's by Margaret Ballard. Before this compilation, there was none at this location for Civil War materials.

[51] Loose Papers, Civil War File, Monroe County Courthouse; Fleming Trainer Service Record, item 2613, M324, Roll 1020, National Archives, Washington, D.C.

died the next day leaving a widow and one or two young children.[52]

The pain of loss reached beyond the death of soldiers. Elizabeth J. Smith was forced to use an attorney to try to regain her lost property once seized by the Monroe Police Guard. Her husband, H. DeWitt Smith of Greenville, fled to Ohio following the proclamation of the Conscription Act.[53]

Augustus Chapman, while still Provost Marshal of Monroe, felt Pauline Ellison was actually gratified by her husband's desertion to the Federal cause. In words that undoubtedly reflected the emotional oratory of early 1862, "I have no doubt that the police are a terror to the disloyal traitors--deserters, horse thiefs, and runaway negroes...."[54]

On July 21st, Lt. Lysander Campbell, Chapman's successor, took over as Provost Marshal of Monroe.[55] William E. Rutledge remembered him.

I was arrested by the Confederate Officers-- Campbell, on account of my union principals [sic] they rebels knew that I aided the Union soldiers that were trying to make their es-

---

[52] Frederick Bahlman, "Down in the Ranks", Journal of the Greenbrier County Historical Society, Vol. II, no. 2, Oct. 1970, 85.

[53] N. Harrison, Attorney, to Maj. Gen. Samuel Jones, ca. July 24, 1863, RG109, M474, Roll 61, National Archives, Washington, D.C.

[54] A.A. Chapman to Maj. Gen. Samuel Jones, June 18, 1863, RG109, M474, roll 61, National Archives.

[55] Ibid.

cape from rebel prison. I did not give any bond or take any oath to obtain my release.[56]

Although not arrested, Rutledge and others were threatened with incarceration in Castle Thunder. Field A. Jarvis claimed that the Provost Marshal threatened several men with imprisonment. It was precisely the fear of prison that held these men together. One thing was now clear, the Confederate authorities knew of the existence of Unionist sympathies in the area that would become Paint Bank.[57]

Monroe County resident Lewis Ballard, imprisoned at Salisbury, escaped in 1863. After days of wandering, Ballard found his way back to Monroe. There were also other civilian and military escapes from the prison at Danville. Union soldiers scrambled from house to house, hoping to find a family willing to aid them.[58]

In the Craig-Alleghany region, the escapees were often successful in reaching the Federal lines. General James Longstreet and his Confederates blocked any hope of reaching Unionist East Tennessee by way of Cumber-

---

[56] Question 19, Henry Tingler testimony, ca. Jan. 9, 1878, in Henry Tingler SCC claim 5006, RG233, M1407, fishe 3221, National Archives, Washington, D.C.

[57] Question 63, Field A. Jarvis testimony, ca. Jan. 9, 1878, in Henry Tingler SCC claim 5006, RG233, M1407, fishe 3221, National Archives, Washington, D.C.; Question 18, Henry Tingler testimony, ca. Jan. 9, 1878, in Henry Tingler SCC claim, National Archives, Washington, D.C.

[58] Morton, Monroe, 306; Ballard, William Ballard, 250-251; Newlin, An Account, 78.

71

land Gap, so Craig and Alleghany Counties became a major escape route to Ohio and beyond. The mountainous terrain and sparse population favored the attempts.[59]

One such famous escape was made by six Federal officers after they fled from the Danville Prison. After two of their number disappeared, they entered Craig County. The soldiers traveled only by night. Figuring where Craig Court House was, the escapees avoided it. In time, they took big chances and entered a private home looking for food.[60]

> We apologized to them for ordering them, in such a manner, to set out supper for us, saying we thought they were 'Secesh'. The woman then called for 'Jim' to come out from under the bed. 'Jim' immediately came forth. On our approach he had hid under the bed, thinking we were Confederate home guards. Jim was a deserter from Buckner's army in East Tennessee.[61]

The woman of the house referred them to another Unionist, James Huffman. When the same escapees reached Huffman's house, they found the door open. Huffman was already a suspected Unionist. A group of home guards searched their home every two weeks. Huffman directed the fleeing Federals to Craig's Creek. Eventually, the soldiers were given the name of William Paxton.[62]

---

[59] Newlin, An Account, 6-7.

[60] Ibid., 77.

[61] Ibid..

[62] Ibid., 78-81.

It was seven miles to Paxton's house, which was situated on the road as it passed over a mountain. After going some four miles on the road, we came to the house where the Rebels congregated. It was near the road, and lights shone from all the windows.[63]

The house described was likely Widow Scott's Tavern, a stop along the James River and Kanawha Turnpike that was a favorite with travelers. Finding William Paxton's house, the escapees felt fortunate that Paxton was present. Paxton asked his two daughters to prepare dinner for the soldiers. Paxton was clear in his sympathies. Only the arrival of a pro-Confederate citizen from Fincastle prevented the soldiers from staying longer.[64]

This new-comer did not seem to notice us until we had finished supper and taken seats before the fire. As I was sitting next him, he took hold of my pants at the knee, and inquired rather roughly, 'Where do you belong?' Not knowing what answer to make, under my circumstances, to such a question, I merely turned my head, and glanced at my three comrades, who in turn looked immediately to the old man Paxton, who very quickly spoke up saying, 'The belong to the 22d, which you know is stationed at the bridge....[65]

---

[63] Ibid., 81.

[64] Ibid., 82-83.

[65] Ibid.

Paxton sent the officers to another loyal Unionist, Mr. Robert Childs. Childs sent them on to Alleghany County resident David Hepler, Sr. Childs expressed concern of new Confederate strategy, "bogus Yankees." These traveling squads tried to intercept Unionists by pretending to be Federal soldiers. In a limited fashion, the tactic had worked. Hepler's son-in-law, Mr. Lewis, was taken in after agreeing to guide some "bogus Yankees" as far as the Greenbrier River.[66]

Other local places were to be avoided by Unionists. Crow's Tavern, sometimes called "Jim Crow's," was a popular tavern that once entertained President Martin Van Buren on vacation. Crow's became a military outpost not unlike Widow Scott's. The Unionist Lewis lived very close to this place.[67]

The officers escaped to Gauley Bridge after crossing the Greenbrier. Such perils were commonplace for the escaped prisoner. The citizens of the region had only their wits to abide by when confronted by often desperate men. As for the ex-prisoner, recapture or exposure threatened them constantly. The "house-to-house" method was moderately successful, and Echols found more Unionist suspects.[68]

If Echols was popular locally, Jones was not. Frequently absent, as his department also contained part of eastern Tennessee, Jones was an "absentee desk general." General Echols found it difficult to work under

---

[66] Ibid, 83, 87-89, 94.

[67] Ibid., 92; Morton, Alleghany, 92.

[68] Newlin, An Account, 98-100; Echols to Seddon, Nov. 8, 1864, OR, Series IV, Vol. 3, 812-814.

such circumstances. He tendered his resignation to Jones in early July 1863. A cache of letters, supporting Echols, flowed in.[69]

Greenbrier County resident Samuel Price wrote Confederate Secretary of War Seddon, "Sir...I have just heard with estream [sic] regret that Genl. John Echols has tendered his resignation, and Iwrite [sic] hurriedly to implore you not to accept it until the end of the campaign...."[70] Augustus Chapman stated while General Jones had accepted Echols' resignation, Seddon should not.[71]

Shortly before the Battle of White Sulphur Springs, a courthouse gathering probably changed Echols' mind. John M. Rowan was among those who expressed dissatisfaction with Jones, citing that one-tenth of his command had not even seen him.[72]

At the very large meeting of the people of the County of Monroe held at the Court House thereof Monday the 17th day of Au-

[69] A.A. Chapman to Seddon, July 4, 1863, RG109, M437, Roll 90, National Archives, Washington, D.C.; Jones' command structure, OR, Vol. 19, Series I, Part 2, 812.

[70] Samuel Price to James A. Seddon, July 3, 1863, RG109, M437, Roll 90, National Archives, Washington, D.C.

[71] A.A. Chapman to James A. Seddon, July 4, 1863, RG109, M437, Roll 90, National Archives, Washington, D.C.

[72] Report from Citizens of Monroe County, Chairman John M. Rowan, ca. Aug. 25, 1863, RG109, M437, Roll 90, National Archives, Washington, D.C.

gust 1863 for the purpose of taking measures for the defence [sic] for this section of Virginia, and especially the County of Monroe it was unanimously agreed to appoint a Committee of Safety for the County whose duty it should be to make general regulations for the defence [sic] of the Country....[73]

By the end of December, Echols felt obligated to explain his actions during the Salem Raid, citing the obscurity of the Rich Patch Road and that his cavalry picket was driven in at Scott's Tavern. Similar explanations did not help Jones. He was finished in this region.[74]

In late 1863, the Unionists had names and faces. Echols needed greater measures. The "bogus Yankees" and increased patrols of the county home guards would frequent the countryside and into the mountains formerly shunned. Aiding Federals would be more difficult, and people would be arrested on much less than fact. The year 1864 held this promise.

[73] Ibid.

[74] Report of Brig. Gen. John Echols to Maj. William B. Myers, Dec. 28, 1863, OR, Chap. 29, part 1, 948-949.

CHAPTER FOUR

THE ELEPHANT HAS ARRIVED--1864

The year 1864 was the year many citizens "saw the elephant."[1] In the past three years, many in the three counties were fortunate enough not to have had actual contact with war. They lived in remote locations not frequented by more than the occasional police patrol. The year 1864 changed most of that. It signaled the year that the Federals actually came in force. The year also revealed the vulnerability of the region.

After Gettysburg, the Eastern Theatre saw many reverses for the Confederacy. Vicksburg fell on July 4, 1863. Confederate General Braxton Bragg was falling back toward the interior of Georgia. Only a victory at Chickamauga Creek temporarily kept the Federals from advancing further. General James Longstreet was sent to Tennessee to aid Bragg.[2]

The war's latest events brought attention to western Virginia, or now, West Virginia. The counties of Monroe and Greenbrier were included due to their geographical location. Both of these counties considered them-

---

[1] The "elephant" is a term for seeing the pandemonium of war and the resultant carnage.

[2] John S. Bowman, ed., The Civil War Day by Day (Greenwich, CT: Brompton Books, 1989) 120; Ibid., 125-126.

selves members of the Old Dominion rather than the new state.[3]

In the spring of 1864, the Federals planned a pronged attack. The main Federal force in the Eastern Theatre was under General Ulysses S. Grant. Grant sent General Franz Sigel down the Shenandoah Valley. General George Crook, the victor of Lewisburg, raided the Virginia and Tennessee Railroad.[4]

The Confederates in the region were under the leadership of General John C. Breckinridge of Kentucky, a former U.S. vice-president under James Buchanan. Breckenridge had the trust of his men and the leadership ability that Jones lacked.[5]

The Federal advance was moving fast in early May. Breckinridge hurriedly assembled his men. Most of the force departed by rail from Jackson River Depot in Alleghany County to the valley town of Staunton. This left most of the Monroe-Craig-Alleghany region open to a raiding party.[6]

The remnants of the Confederate command fell to Brigadier General Albert Gallatin Jenkins. General Crook marched from Charleston and battled Jenkins at Cloyd's Mountain on May 9th. Jenkins was mortally wounded in this battle, and Crook destroyed a portion of the Virginia and Tennessee Railroad. Knowing Breckin-

---

[3] Morton, Monroe, 156.

[4] William C. Davis, The Battle of New Market, 20.

[5] Ibid., 16.

[6] Johnston, Captain Beirne Chapman and Chapman's Battery, 19.

with V-Rad list of

scanned into EPIC.

urned on and ready for the day

4 memory.

stations are up and running.

ure all equipment is returned to
olies are put away. Check/charge

if not already done by 3rd shift.

on to the network

e able to do everything on the list ~
been accomplished. All tasks must
noted. Please put the list, when

g the department ready for the day!

ridge would soon return, Crook turned back toward Monroe County.[7]

Averell, who had taken a different route, was trying to link up with Crook's main force. Averell found himself in a bad situation, as he had in the Salem Raid. His troops were hungry and harried, and they did not enjoy the success they had that previous winter. Taking obscure roads once again, the Federals rode toward the Paint Bank area.[8]

By May 14, Crook passed Sweet Springs Mountain. His men camped along Indian Creek in Monroe County and occupied Beverly Ballard's property. Near Willow Bend, a bushwhacker named Bickman was turned over to the men of the 36th Ohio Infantry. He was quickly shot, and a note was pinned to his body which said, "This is the fate of all bushwhackers."[9]

In similar fashion, Union was quickly occupied. Reverend Houston claimed Union soldiers "desolated" Walnut Grove, the home of Oliver Beirne. Beirne's livestock were killed and eaten by the soldiers. Confederate General "Mudwall" Jackson did not have enough men to battle Crook openly. As his only option, Jackson

---

[7] Howard Rollins McManus, The Battle of Cloyds Mountain--The Virginia and Tennessee Railroad Raid, April 29-May 19, 1864, 10; Ibid., 21; Ibid., 37; Ibid., 49.

[8] McManus, The Battle of Cloyds Mountain, 66; Ibid., 75.

[9] Patricia Givens Johnson, The U.S. Army Invades the New River Valley, (Christiansburg, VA: Walpa Publishing, 1986), 87; Question 19, Beverly Ballard testimony, in Beverly Ballard SCC claim 16145, RG233, M1407, National Archives, Washington, D.C.

monitored the Federals. A Union picket attempted to lure hungry Confederates by ringing cowbells, but when the Confederates showed up in force, the picket disappeared.[10]

Further east, on the ride up Potts' Mountain, Averell came across Jackson's wagon train. At the home of John Starks on top of the mountain, a wedding was in progress. Among the guests was Unionist Leonard Hellems. As the cavalry passed, they took the horse belonging to Hellems. The next day Hellems met one of Averell's staff officers. Hellems explained that he was a Union man. The officer offered to bring him to see Averell. Hellems accepted, but enroute, the order came to march.[11]

> I rode the hors [sic] there and when he was taken, I went to the officer and asked him if he could not get me back my brother's horse--he said he could not--as the horse had gone on but if I had of come sooner he would have gone to the Gen. and obtained the horse for me. I am a cripple and I rode the horse my brother walked and hitched the horse when we got to the house of a mate by

---

[10] Johnson, The U.S. Army Invades, 89; Morton, Monroe, Houston Diary, May 15, 1864, 178.

[11] McManus, The Battle of Cloyds Mountain, 73; Question No. 79, Leonard Hellems testimony, in Leonard Hellems SCC claim 16849, RG 233, M1407, fishe 4088, National Archives, Washington, D.C.

the name of Starks. We went there with several others to witness a marriage....[12]

Averell's exhausted troops met up with Crook, whose encampment stretched for miles, from the north side of the town of Union into the farmland. Said one of Crook's soldiers, "While marching through Union there was a Sabbath stillness, scarcely anyone to be seen." Later it was learned that many citizens and farmers residing near the town took most of their possessions and livestock into the hills.[13]

The Federals retreated quickly westward, their mission fulfilled. The compaign threw open the lines, and some civilians left the Confederacy. Allen Armentrout crossed the Ohio River into Gallia County. Freedman Allen Campbell, who had lived near James Hogshead's farm several miles from Second Creek, went with Crook's men to Ohio. After his arrival there, Campbell worked in the Pomeroy Saltworks for several years. Afraid of being forced to fight, Campbell could not stay.[14]

The seeds of Unionism grew. Susannah Abbott, of Craig County, had a U.S. flag draped about the coffin of

---

[12] Question No. 74, William Hellems testimony, in Leonard Hellems SCC claim, RG233, M1407, fishe 4088, National Archives.

[13] McManus, The Battle of Cloyds Mountain, 75; Johnson, The U.S. Army Invades, 88 [from E.C. Arthur's "The Dublin Raid," The Ohio Soldier, Jan. 5 and Apr. 13, 1889].

[14] Bostic Interview, Oct. 1988; Question 4, testimony dated Feb. 4, 1873, Entry 732, in Allen Campbell SCC Claim 19343, RG217, Box 409, National Archives, Washington, D.C.; Ibid., Question 79.

her husband, John. Around the Back Valley, a serious Unionist group formed. William E. Rutledge claimed that a Union soldier named Williams approached several farmers in the area. Rutledge and Leonard Hellems were assuredly members of the organization.[15]

> There was a society called the Loyal League that had for its object the promotion of the Union sentiment and signs & passwords by which we could tell one another it came to from the Union Army a man by the name of Williams organized a Chapter of it in our neighborhood. Mr. Helms belonged to this league for I was at one of its meetings when he was initiated.[16]

Others that may have been members were Washington Jarvis, Field A. Jarvis, George A. Linton, and Henry Tingler. Other names mentioned as possible Unionists

---

[15] Remarks Section, Summary Report, n.d., Entry 732, in Susannah Abbott SCC claim 14702, RG 217, Box 343, National Archives, Washington, D.C.; Question 65, William E. Rutledge testimony, ca. Oct. 4, 1872, in Hellems SCC claim, RG233, M1407, fishe 4088, National Archives, Washington, D.C.
It was said that Abbott has been a member of the "Union League," which could have been the same organization that the Paint Bankers were in. The U.S. flag was given to Susannah Abbott by Mr. Joel Custer, a local resident who was with the 7th WV Cavalry in late 1864 and 1865. Colonel Otey of that regiment gave Custer the flag. John Abbott died after the Civil War, in July, 1865.

[16] Question 65, William E. Rutledge testimony, ca. Oct. 4, 1872, in Hellems SCC claim, RG233, M1407, fishe 4088, National Archives, Washington, D.C.

were Abraham Armentrout and Andrew Wilson. George A. Linton stated,

> ...it was generally know Abe Armentrout Allen J. Armentrout Field A. Jarvis William Rutledge Washington Jarvis they could testify as to his [Henry Tingler] loyalty...the list above were the most prominent Union men in the neighborhood, where we lived was know through out the county as the "Union Hole."[17]

If there had not been an organized group up to that time, there now was. Crook's men had assured that. Whether the Loyal League was a branch of the Order of the Heroes of America was uncertain. The traditions were similar. One of the members of the Order was a Christiansburg wheelwright named Williams. It is not known if this was the same Williams Back Valley residents spoke of in context with the Loyal League.[18]

---

[17] Question 60 and 61, n.d., George A. Linton Testimony, in Tingler SCC claim, RG233, M1407, fishe 3221, National Archives, Washington, D.C.

[18] Report of Detectives, Oct. 10, 1864, OR, Series IV, Vol. 3, 807.

The Heroes of America, according to Professor J.G. de Roulhac Hamilton ("The Heroes of America," Southern History Association, Washington, D.C., Vol. 11, 1907), was confined to whites and the "red strings" was an imitation of the Bible tale of Rahab. As there were a great many Union sympathizers in western North Carolina, western Virginia, and east Tennessee, the secret society was formed to protect these people and their families. It was a consolidated opposition to the policies

While the loyalties were becoming more sharply defined, Breckinridge's men routed Sigel's Federals at New Market on May 15th. Grant's men engaged in heavy fighting at the Wilderness and Spotsylvania Court House. Despite ugly losses, Grant kept marching towards Richmond.[19]

After New Market, the ineffective Sigel was replaced by Major General David Hunter. Hunter wasted little time and marched his men down the Shenandoah Valley, burning several buildings in Lexington. Some of Breckinridge's men had been fighting at Cold Harbor with Lee's main force. Upon Hunter's threat, these soldiers were forced to return to the Shenandoah Valley by rail. Confederate reinforcements arrived just in time to fight off Hunter's men at Lynchburg. Badly demoralized, the Federals retreated westward. Following the James River and Kanawha Turnpike, they hurried through Craig County.[20]

One New Castle resident, David Zimmerman, used hand signals that made Federal officers realize that he was a Unionist. Zimmerman belonged to the Union Party and was not afraid of revealing himself to the Fed-

---

of the Confederacy and did not seem to restrict itself by emphasizing any one policy.

[19] Bowman, ed., The Civil War Day by Day, 160-161.

[20] Johnston, Captain Beirne Chapman and Chapman's Battery, 22-24; Jane Echols Johnston and Brenda Lynn Williams, Hard Times, 1861-1865, Volume II (New Castle, VA: Craig Co. Historical Society, 1990), 149.

erals. The Federals could do little for Zimmerman, as they had to keep moving.[21]

Other Unionists had contact with the fleeing Federal army. As William Paxton walked to work at Widow Scott's Tavern, he noticed a contingent of Federals on the Turnpike. Upon seeing Paxton, and thinking him a Confederate guerrilla, the soldiers fired a few rounds in his direction. Paxton turned around and fled back to his home.[22]

Hunter's men passed quickly by Sweet Springs and westward. Once safely behind their lines, the Federals had to be transported by rail back to the lower Shenandoah Valley. Hunter was soon replaced by Crook.[23]

Confederates streamed down the Shenandoah Valley and took the offensive without any opposition. Lee was still in desperate shape. He faced Grant's main forces. Lee let Jubal Early use a free hand in pushing into Federal territory to take the pressure off. By the next month, Early's forces defeated a makeshift Federal force under General Lew Wallace at the Monocacy River in Maryland. The Confederates camped at the home of Lincoln cabinet member Montgomery Blair and helped themselves to stored paper currency.[24]

---

[21] last page, Petition of David Zimmerman, June 24, 1871, RG233, M1407, fishe 4829, National Archives, Washington, D.C.

[22] Question 18, William Paxton testimony, Sept. 1872, in William Paxton SCC claim, RG123, National Archives, Washington, D.C.

[23] Johnston, Captain Beirne Chapman and Chapman's Battery, 25; Cohen, Civil War in West Virginia, 105.

[24] Ibid., 25-29.

Realizing Grant would not let them stay at Washington's doorstep for very long, Early launched an assault on Fort Stevens. The Confederates soon withdrew after no progress was made. Crook's newly formed troops pursued Early into Loudoun County. At Kernstown, on July 24th, Crook's army was soundly defeated.[25]

In the Alleghany-Craig-Monroe region, Unionism was a hot topic. The Confederate military forces remained far up the Shenandoah Valley or with Lee's main force now around Petersburg. The responsibility for rooting out the Unionists called for the county police to fend for themselves. The Confederacy's manpower was strained to its limits.

Some families had to split up to stay alive with renewed police searches. Such was the case with the Jarvis Family. Several of the family decided to go to Gallia County, Ohio. A few cousins were already there, and area families had been migrating to Gallia since the early 1800's. Although Field and his nephew George Linton stayed, Field's two sons, John and Morgan Jarvis, would have to go. Along with them went George's brother, James N. Linton; his sister Sena Linton; and his mother (and Field's sister) Susannah Linton. None of those who left would ever move back.[26]

---

[25] Ibid., 28-30.

[26] Bostic Interview, Oct. 1988; Gallia Co. Historical Society, Cemeteries of Springfield Township (Gallipolis, OH: Gallia Co. Historical Society, 1979), 22; Ibid., 24; Ibid., 39.

Other area families that went to Gallia were the Roses, Prewitts, Stulls, Bostics, and Armentrouts.

Changes also occurred in other area families. William Paxton had married again. His second wife, Elizabeth Jane Reynolds, was twenty-five years his junior. They married on May 8, 1864, and would eventually have eight children. Paxton, not anxious to have the war find him again, moved north to a farm in Alleghany County.[27]

Other counties exerted pressure on Unionist residents. The Montgomery County Committee of Safety, concerned about the presence of active Unionists, called on Confederate Commissioner Henry J. Leory. In August 1864, Leory sent detectives from Richmond into western Virginia to locate the whereabouts of key Unionist leaders. Members of the Order of the Heroes of America told the detectives, who were on their travels in Botetourt and Montgomery Counties, that there were members of the Order in the Confederate Army. A majority of the 54th Virginia and the 22nd Virginia were such members.[28]

While in Christiansburg, Leory's detectives came across a Dunkard preacher who said it was a fine thing that most of the 22nd had deserted. Some members of the Order were county officials in Montgomery and Washington Counties. It is less likely that this was so in the Monroe-Alleghany-Craig region.[29]

---

[27] Lucy B. Hurst Family Sheets, Roanoke, VA; Harvey B. Rose Letter, Nov. 2, 1923, in Manerva Reynolds Pension, Act of 1902, Virginia State Archives.

[28] Report of Detectives, Oct. 10, 1864, OR, Series IV, Vol. 3, 806-809; Ibid., 811.

[29] Tatum, Disloyalty in the Confederacy, 163; Report of Detectives, OR, Series IV, Vol. 3, 807.

General Echols, long interested in eliminating the Unionist element in the population, wrote to Confederate Secretary of War Seddon,

> We have for some time back suspected the existence of a secret treasonable association, but have not until recently been able to determine its existence and extent, when Mr. Leory, by his intelligence and perseverance, has been enabled to certainty its character and existence and extent.[30]

Leory continued his probe. The new focus was on the Heroes of America. Knowledge of its existence in western Virginia was not discovered until the autumn of 1864, and far too late to be of any service to the Confederacy.[31]

Leory's detectives kept probing. At one point, Leory stated in a letter to Seddon,

> Within ten miles of this place we find three justices of the peace and one Methodist minister attached to the society....I am told there are 800 members of the order in Montgomery County alone.[32]

Leory sent his detectives into Alleghany County in late 1864. They found some Unionists.[33]

---

[30] Brig. Gen. John Echols to James A. Seddon, Sept. 1, 1864, OR, Series IV, Vol. 3, 805.

[31] Ibid., 805-806; Tatum, Disloyalty in the Confederacy, 33.

[32] Henry J. Leory to James A. Seddon, Sept. 20, 1864, OR, Series IV, Vol. 3, 806.

[33] Ibid.

Those citizens who left for war were in as much or greater danger. On June 20, 1864, Andrew Cambel Reynolds fell seriously ill with dysentery. Only ten days before, Reynolds had enlisted in the 28th Virginia Infantry at Gaines Mill. A grueling march to the Bermuda Hundred line followed. After little or no action around the Clay Farm, Reynolds and several others in his company fell ill.[34]

After some three months in Chimborazo Hospital Number One in Richmond, Reynolds went home on a three-month furlough. Reynolds visited his mother, Mary Jane Goode Reynolds, at her home near Lexington. Reynolds felt well enough to see his fiancee. Manerva Ann Rose, daughter of Jackson Rose, was at the family's home. The three months were soon over.[35]

Reynolds started back to Petersburg. In Alleghany County, he stopped to visit his sister, "Lyda" Paxton, the second wife of William Paxton. Paxton had serious reservations about young Cambel's health should he return to the Confederate Army. Paxton told the young man that Lee had surrendered. Young Reynolds was advised to seek work in the westernmost portions of Virginia. Paxton had heard there were paying jobs along the Ohio

[34] Frank Fields, <u>28th Virginia Infantry</u>, 76; Wallace, <u>Guide to Virginia Military Organizations</u>, 111; Form No. 5, Apr. 26, 1923, Manerva Reynolds Pension Record, Act of 1902, Confederate Pension Applications, Virginia State Archives, Richmond, VA; Thomas J. Howe, <u>Wasted Valor--The Petersburg Campaign</u> (Lynchburg, VA: H.E. Howard, 1988), 79.

[35] Harvey B. Rose letter, Nov. 2, 1923, Manerva Reynolds Pension Record, Act of 1902, Confederate Pension Applications, Virginia State Archives.

River. Reynolds took Paxton at his word and never returned to the lines. Several months later Paxton's loyalty was clear. His first son's name was Joseph Abraham Lincoln Paxton.[36]

Other citizens showed their loyalty to the United States in alternative ways. Upon reaching Gallia County, John Jarvis enlisted in the Federal army. Jarvis joined Company K, 173rd Ohio Infantry, under Captain James Marcum, on September 15, 1864. Jarvis' unit quickly marched to Nashville, Tennessee. Although held in reserve to General Steadman's command, the 173rd was present, but not engaged, in the battle there on December 15-17. Morgan would soon follow his brother's footsteps.[37]

Late 1864 was a hard time for most mountain yeoman farmers in the region. The last year had seen bad weather, thievery by soldiers and civilians of both sides, and "tax-in-kind" payments which further depleted badly needed resources. Even the Jarvis' property was lean. Field had only a few sheep, an "indifferent" bed, an old desk, and a set of blacksmith tools.[38]

Desertion was running high. On December 14, 1864, Fleming Trainer signed the oath to the United States at Charleston. Although Jackson Rose's son-in-

---

[36] Ibid.; Lucy B. Hurst Family Group Sheets, Roanoke, VA.

[37] Declaration of Invalid Pension, John E. Jarvis, 695530, RG15, National Archives, Washington, D.C.

[38] Summary of Material Facts, Feb. 2, 1880, in Field A. Jarvis, National Archives; Ella Lonn, PhD, Desertion During the Civil War (New York: Century Co., 1928), 13.

law had deserted the 60th Virginia in Giles county back in September 1863, he came forward only now.[39]

Early's Confederates were also lean. A crushing defeat at the Third Battle of Winchester on September 19th left several local heroes dead. George Patton of the 22nd Virginia and Augustus Chapman's son, George Beirne Chapman, were among the casualties. General Philip Sheridan, now the Federal commander in the region, held onto Winchester and set fire to many vital crops. While Sheridan was away, Early launched a surprise attack on the Federals at Middletown on October 19th. For a time the attack was successful; however, the hungry soldiers were more interested in capturing the foodstuffs they craved, and the delays proved disastrous. Therefore, food won the Battle of Cedar Creek. Temptation proved too great, and the survival instinct so inherent in Unionists was strongest of all.[40]

Back in Monroe, the county scrambled to keep the families of Confederate soldiers supplied. M. McDaniel, on December 20, 1864, provided the following: 1,817 bushels of wheat, 65 bushels of whey, 10 bushels of corn, 924 bushels of pork, 1,102 bushels of beef. Among the families mentioned were those of James Bostick (2 people--Jane and son Marion), Alexander Bostick

---

[39] Item 2613, Fleming Trainer Service Record, muster roll dated Oct. 31, 1863, RG109, M324, Roll 1020, National Archives, Washington, D.C.; Ibid, Loyalty Oath, Dec. 14, 1864.

[40] Johnston, Captain Beirne Chapman and Chapman's Battery, 35; Ibid., 40.

(7 people) of the 60th Virginia, and William Pritt (3 people) of the same unit.[41]

Area veterans showed unusual valor during the war's last months. N. Augustus Dunbar, at Cedar Creek, captured a 3-inch rifle cannon and took it off the field under fire. The piece remained with his regiment until the war closed. John B. Linton fell with a wound in the left hip at Lynchburg, and only the efforts of a fellow soldier saved him from almost certain death. Linton lay outside the Confederate trenches unable to move. An officer dragged him back. Linton returned home on furlough by October 31st.[42]

Despite the brave efforts, the Confederates lost ground. Atlanta had fallen, and Federal General William Tecumseh Sherman crossed the State of Georgia and completed his famous march to the sea. He devastated many of the vital railroad ties in the lower South. Grant's army besieged Petersburg, and those long lines of trench works were similar to those of Vicksburg. Lincoln was re-elected in the autumn elections. Everywhere the Confederates were fraying.

As 1864 finished, Leory's men made some arrests in western Virginia. Lieutenant Colonel Charles S. Pey-

---

[41] Loose Papers, Civil War File, Monroe County Court House.

[42] Confederate Veteran, Vol. XXXIII, No. 5, 187; Disability by Wound Form 1, John B. Linton Confederate Pension Application, Act of 1902, Roll 86 (Richmond, VA: filmed by the Genealogical Society of Salt Lake City, Utah, 1990), Virginia State Archives, Richmond, VA; Johnston and Williams, Hard Times 1861-1865, Vol. II, 291.

ton commanded the men who made the arrests. Rich Patch resident Jesse Humphries was arrested for harboring deserters. Humphries was sent to Wythe County along with Zeb Persinger, William Persinger, and William Quickel. One reason Humphries was not liked was due to the fact he was a member of the northern branch of the Methodist Church. In post-war years, Humphries stated others in the Rich Patch were also Unionists. He named Isaac Wolf, Nancy Persinger, John C. Smith, Nash Persinger (who was a Confederate soldier), Harvey Humphries, William N. Fridley, Richard Fridley, Charles K. Humphries, George P. King, and George M. Jamison among others.[43]

The year 1864 clarified the desperation. Whole communities now defied the hold of the Confederacy. Soldiers could only think of their families far away.

---

[43] George Stull, Harvey Persinger, and Isaac Fridley to Adjutant of Western District of Virginia, Jan. 3, 1865, RG109, M437, Roll 149, National Archives, Washington, D.C.; Remarks Section, Summary Report, Dec. 5, 1877, Entry 732, in Charles L. Humphries adm. for SCC claim of Jesse Humphries, RG217, Box 339, National Archives; Louise Collins Perkins, "Some Residents Supported the North," Virginian Review, Wed., June 6, 1989; Decision by Henry Leory, Jan. 27, 1865, RG109, M437, Roll 149, National Archives; Decision by Leory, Feb. 10, 1865, RG109, M437, Roll 149, National Archives; Decision by Leory, Feb. 3, 1865, RG109, M437, Roll 149, National Archives.

CHAPTER FIVE

SWORDS INTO PLOWSHARES--1865

The year 1865 promised very little for those starving Confederates and their families. The thin lines in Petersburg were open to attack in the spring. Many of Early's soldiers left to be with their families. Those who remained experienced total defeat at Waynesboro, Virginia, in February. Sherman was in the Carolinas. Columbia burned, and the remnants of General Joseph Johnston's Confederates could do little to stop Sherman.[1]

In January and February of 1865, John E. Jarvis, resided in the town of Columbia, Tennessee. Federal Colonel Sheppard made a forced march in which Jarvis was a victim of exposure and possibly abuse. Sergeant Thomas G. Griffith of Lawrence County, Ohio, and a member of John's regiment, saw John shortly upon his return.[2]

> I saw him when he cum [sic] back and after they had taken him to the regimental hospital for treatment at Johnson vill [sic]

---

[1] Johnston, <u>Captain Beirne Chapman and Chapman's Battery</u>, 41.

[2] Sgt. Thomas G. Griffith testimony, Feb. 14, 1892, in John E. Jarvis Pension record, RG15, National Archives.

Tenn....beating around his face, and it settled in his eye.[3]

John suffered from a weak back and neuralgia of the head for the rest of his life. Morgan fared worse.[4]

Among the Jarvis family, another relative met tragedy. George Linton's youngest sister, Seth, had married Nash Persinger of Alleghany County. Sometime during the war, the couple moved to Putnam County, West Virginia. Nash enlisted in the Confederate Army. Once Putnam County fell under federal occupation, Seth found it hard to see her husband. As she tried to cross the lines, she was mortally wounded by a Union picket.[5]

One Jarvis in Gallia County followed his brother. Morgan Jarvis was only 18 years old in 1865. On February 13, 1865, Morgan enlisted as a private in Company C, 194th Ohio. Described by descendants as a humorous and clever boy, Morgan epitomized the real tragedy of the American Civil War. From Portsmouth, Ohio, the company, led by Gallia resident Captain Benjamin Martin, marched to Jefferson County, West Virginia. After a time in Charlestown, Morgan became sick.[6]

---

[3] Ibid.

[4] Statement before Notary Public, Jan. 25, 1892, in John E. Jarvis Pension record, RG15, National Archives.

[5] Persinger Family Group Sheets, Nora B. Martin, Newport News, VA.

[6] Pension Certificate Receipt, Adjutant General's Office, Feb. 18, 1879, in Field A. Jarvis Pension, RG15, National Archives; "Roll of Honor of Ohio Soldiers" in Official Roster of the Soldiers of the State of Ohio in the War of the Rebellion, Vol. X (Cincinnati: Ohio Roster Commission, 1889), 674.

Morgan was sent to the hospital at Harper's Ferry and later to Cumberland, Maryland. There he spoke to a member of the U.S. Christian Commission, George W. Connaway. Morgan knew he was dying and requested his personal items be sent to his parents. He informed Field and Sallie Jarvis that he was not afraid to die. Morgan Taylor Jarvis died of typhoid fever on April 14, 1865.[7]

Connaway wrote Field and Sallie a letter of his conversation with Morgan. As it was tricky to communicate with a family so far away, Captain Martin wrote Morgan's cousin, Frank Glenn.[8]

> Morgan was a good Boy and a good Soldier and I mourn his death almost as much as anyone can....Sometime since then was a letter came to my care for him and I have just opened and read it and find it is from his brother who is in the Army but no directions where to write to him.[9]

Glenn in turn found John Jarvis. His description of Morgan's death is a fine example of compassion.

---

[7] George W. Connaway to Field and Sallie Jarvis, Apr. 15, 1865, in Field A. Jarvis Pension, National Archives; Pension Certificate Receipt, Adjutant General's Office, Feb. 18, 1879, in Field A. Jarvis Pension, RG15, National Archives.

[8] Connaway to Jarvis, Apr. 15, 1865, in Field A. Jarvis Pension, National Archives; Capt. Benjamin Martin to Frank Glenn, Apr. 26, 1865, in Field A. Jarvis Pension, National Archives.

[9] Martin to Glenn, Apr. 26, 1865, in Field A. Jarvis Pension, National Archives.

der Cosin [sic] after so long a time I am...to let you no [sic] that Morgan Jarvis is ded [sic]. I was sorry to here [sic] that Morgan was a clever boy...his nuse [sic] wrote to his parents often he died he says he was willing to dye [sic] well. John we have all got to dye [sic] its a good thing to bee [sic] reddy [sic].[10]

Connaway's letter was as poignant, if not as heartfelt, to the parents of the dead boy.

I take my pen in hand to in form you of the sad news of the Deth [sic] of your sun [sic] he was taken sick and sent to Harpers Fary [sic] Hospital and then sent up here to Cumberland Md. he came here on the 9th of this month and he died on the 12th. he requested me to wright [sic] to you after his deth [sic] and let you now [sic] it he sent for one of the Christian Commissioners to come and see him.[11]

If this was an epitaph for Morgan, it was just as applicable to the Confederacy. Petersburg fell in April. Lee's meager army could no longer hold back the Federals. Richmond was abandoned by the Confederate administration. Lee's men surrendered at Appomattox Court House, cut off and exhausted. Johnston later surrendered in North Carolina, and Confederate General Kirby Smith held out in Texas until late May.

---

[10] Frank Glenn to John E. Jarvis, May 26, 1865, Field A. Jarvis Pension, National Archives.

[11] Connaway to Jarvis, Apr. 15, 1865, in Field A. Jarvis Pension, National Archives.

In Monroe, S.R. Houston reported in his diary:

April 15--Soldiers returning and some horses disappearing. Thieves pretend to be impressing them for the war. A great deal of excitement, apprehending evils from the Yankees and the disbanded soldiers, who are far from home without current money and without provisions. Our condition is at present truly lamentable.[12]

It was lamentable. Thousands of exhausted soldiers did not know what they would come home to. James Bostic came home dispirited. He put his cap on the head of his young son. The boy ran off to play with some friends, and, when asked who had given him the cap, he pointed at his father and said, "that man over there!"[13]

Citizen-soldiers became citizens again. It was the last time the militia system would be used in such a manner. Its ineffective nature in a crisis situation would bring its demise. Talk arose of a general amnesty for Confederate soldiers. S.R. Houston wrote on April 20,

A letter from A.T. Caperton produced quite an excitement this evening. The legislature and other public men are requested to meet upon terms of peace. Very liberal terms are offered by President Lincoln....[14]

However, the death of Lincoln brought harsh terms to the Reconstruction period. Before Houston wrote that entry

---

[12] Morton, <u>Monroe</u>, Houston Diary, Apr. 15, 1865, 179.

[13] Bostic Interview, Oct., 1988.

[14] Morton, <u>Monroe</u>, Houston Diary, Apr. 20, 1865, 179.

in his diary, Lincoln had become the victim of an assassin's bullet. S.R. Houston noted sadly, "Mr. Caperton returned from Staunton. Nothing accomplished. President Lincoln's death arrested their discussion."[15] The whole region, and the whole country, was in shock.

Alleghany County fared little better. Someone noted on April 17th, "A good deal of felony is reported."[16] The County Court used up all means of feeding the citizens until the autumn. Thompson McAllister was asked to purchase grain abroad. The distributors would only accept specie, and no Confederate money.[17]

What became of the Unionists? They melted into the population. After the war, they might have resented their treatment. Most did not. Who was to enforce the finger pointing of the war's many atrocities against them? For the Southern Unionists, it was not victory. The Unionists simply swallowed a bitter pill before the rest of the South did.

The whole country had to start again. Those brave soldiers came home. Those men who had been brave enough to state their convictions adjusted their lives to the mainstream. A hundred years of wartime side-effects occurred.

---

[15] Ibid., Apr. 25, 1865, 179.

[16] Morton, <u>Alleghany</u>, 55.

[17] Ibid.

AFTERWARD--REMEMBERING

What became of the people that made this history complete? Many were anxious to get back to farming and the lives they knew so well. Others were more reluctant to do so. All of their lives were changed by what happened to them in the Civil War. The Jarvis Family and its relations were such a family. Field A. grew steadily poorer, culminating in monetary difficulties with his nephew Frank Neel. Field collected a pension for Morgan's service.[1] Sallie Jarvis died,

> ...on the 10th inst. at her late home on Potts' Creek, of pneumonia, Mrs. Sarah Jarvis, an exemplary member of the M.E. Church, in the 80th year of her age. [In reality it was in 65][2]

Field himself died on April 14, 1890. He was 90 years old. The Monroe Watchman called him one of the "landmarks" of the county. William M. Hellems of Paint Bank simply put in his diary, "April 14, 1890--Fieldon Jarvis died."[3]

---

[1] Clerk's Notation, Sept. 20, 1879, in Field A. Jarvis Pension, National Archives.

[2] C.M. Johnston, ed., Border Watchman, Apr. 28, 1876, Vol. 5, No. 14, 3.

[3] William M. Hellems Diary, Apr. 14, 1890, typescript; A.S. Johnston, ed., Monroe Watchman, Apr. 23, 1890, Vol. 19, No. 12, 1.

Field's children lived well into the 20th century. John never returned to live in West Virginia. Upon his release from service, he married Mary Drake of Ohio. He settled for a time in Pike County, Ohio. In the mid-1880's, John moved to Missouri. In 1890 he lived in Gainesville, Texas, near his nephew, Wilbur C. Bostic, third son of James and Jane Bostic. After the Bostics left to go home to West Virginia about 1893, John moved to Pottawottomie County, Oklahoma, where he died in 1907.[4]

Winnifred and Matilda Jarvis never married. In her latter years, Matilda was wheelchair bound. They lived in their parents' house with unmarried brother Joseph. They raised the oldest of their sister's children, Marion. Later, they raised Marion's daughter Lelia. Both sisters died within several months of each other in 1923. Joseph was shuffled about from home to home until October 1927, when he was found dead in the road leading to Paint Bank.[5]

Jane would survive her husband by forty-one years. James Bostic, while doing chores in bad weather, came down with pneumonia and died on May 17, 1886, at the age of 47. Jane would survive both of her daughters and one of her sons. She was living with her son

---

[4] Bostic Interview, Apr. 1988; Marriage Statement, May 5, 1898, in John E. Jarvis Pension 695530, RG15, National Archives; Ibid., Declaration of Pension, Mar. 2, 1907.

[5] Bostic Interview, Apr., 1988; Layman Reynolds Interview, Sept. 1991.

Wilbur when she died on August 26, 1927. She was one day shy of her 91st birthday.[6]

George Linton lived with James and Jane Bostic after the war. He and James would do much together. Linton became something of a preacher and stayed with Jane after James died. George died on November 4, 1910, at the age of 84. James and Sena died before George.[7]

Their kin, the James N. Linton Family, lived about as long. John B. Linton lived the longest, dying on August 25, 1924, at 80 years of age. Susan Linton died in 1906. Susan's siblings, Euphemie and William, passed away in 1911. Both of the latter died in the house in which they were born.[8]

William Rutledge remained in Paint Bank. Hellem's diary has his death date as December 16, 1885. Before Rutledge died, he was able to give detailed information of the Paint Bank Unionists. Henry Tingler died January 22, 1910. His mill still stands today, largely

---

[6] Bostic and Reynolds, grave list of Bostic Cemetery; Bostic Interview, Jan. 1990.

[7] Ruby B. Linton Interview, Clifton Forge, VA, Mar. 1990; Bostic and Reynolds grave list of Bostic Cemetery; Gallia Co. Historical Society, Cemeteries of Springfield Township, 22; A.S. Johnston, ed., Monroe Watchman, Dec. 15, 1910, Vol. 39, No. 45, 1.

[8] Bostic and Reynolds, grave list of Bostic Cemetery; A.S. Johnston, ed., Monroe Watchman, June 8, 1911, Vol. 40, No. 19, 1.

thanks to the preservation efforts of one of his descendants.[9]

William Paxton lived a long time after the war. James Huffman wrote one of the Federal officers that they had aided in 1867 that Paxton "is living yet." Towards the end of his long life, Paxton secured a Southern Claims Commission pension. He died on January 9, 1900, aged 86 years.[10]

Andrew Cambel Reynolds lived a year on the Ohio River. Reynolds returned and married Manervy Ann Rose. A fiddler, Cambel was offered much money to play at dances. Manervy told her children that she did not want them to vote Democratic because they "killed her daddy." Cambel died near Paint Bank on December 7, 1911. Manervy lived on until 1932. A pension from the State of Virginia was granted Manervy in 1923.[11]

Frank F. Neel was a magistrate for some 18 years. Neel owned a farm on Indian Creek. His son, Allen A.P. Neel became an army chaplain during the war

---

[9] Hellems Diary, Dec. 16, 1885; Ibid., Jan. 22, 1910; William E. Rutledge testimony, undated, in Tingler SCC claim, National Archives.

[10] Newlin, An Account, 7; Lucy B. Hurst-Paxton Family Group Sheets.

[11] Bostic Interview, Apr. 1990; Thurmon Reynolds Interview, July 1990; Application for a Widow of a Confederate Soldier, May 12, 1923, in Manerva Reynolds Pension, Act of 1918, Virginia State Archives; A.S. Johnston, ed., Monroe Watchman, Dec. 28, 1911, Vol. 40, No. 48, 1; J.M. Johnston, ed., Monroe Watchman, Nov. 10, 1932, Vol. 61, No. 40, 1.

(1862). Frank died in 1896, and Allen was alive in 1903.[12]

Sarah Wiley, mother of A.B. Wiley, was 91 years old in 1881, when she complained in a letter of the fate of her pension. She claimed that her grandson stole the money. Whether true or not, it was a sad ending to a sad story.[13]

Henderson Reed, comrade of James A. Bostic, moved to Kansas. Last of a family of 16 children, his first wife died in 1882 in West Virginia. Upon his second marriage in 1885, he moved to Kansas. He died in Overbrook, Kansas, on September 17, 1917, aged 81 years.[14]

Jesse Humphries died before he could collect his Southern Claims Commission pension in 1871. His son William continued the struggle to obtain it. Aaron and Zebediah Persinger were released by Leory after taking an oath of allegiance in February 1865.[15]

Ruth Rose lived in the Craig County area until her death on May 27, 1891. Many of her children moved to Gallia County. Among those who stayed were Manervy

---

[12] Comstock, ed., West Virginia Heritage Encyclopedia, Supplemental No. 1, 107; Scott, Lowry's, Bryan's, and Chapman's Batteries, 103.

[13] Sarah Wiley to officials, July 14, 1881, in Sarah Wiley Pension 186977, RG15, National Archives.

[14] A.S. Johnston, ed., Monroe Watchman, Oct. 11, 1917, Vol. 46, No. 37, 1.

[15] Remarks Section, Summary Report, Dec. 5, 1877, Entry 732, in Jesse Humphries SCC claim, Box 339, National Archives; Decision by Leory, Feb. 10, 1865, RG109, M437, Roll 149, National Archives.

Reynolds and Harvey Brown Rose, who lived until 1926.[16]

Allen Armentrout returned to West Virginia. He died August 17, 1889, near Paint Bank. His father, Abraham Armentrout, died January 4, 1893. Abraham's wife, Bethsaida Armentrout (sister of widow Ruth Rose) died on December 7, 1894. Abraham Lincoln Armentrout, Allen's oldest son, moved to the Gap Mills area. The second son, Lafayette, married one of the Bostic daughters, Emma. After Emma died of childbirth complications in 1893, Armentrout remarried and left for Centralia, Missouri. He died there in 1913.[17]

Of the more famous regional figures, Augustus A. Chapman died in 1876. Chapman died on a journey to Charleston to nominate a friend for the office of governor. Three of his sons preceded him. Allen T. Caperton, in 1876, was elected to the United States Senate. He died in office on July 26, 1877. Thompson McAllister of Alleghany died in 1871.[18]

The numerous other military and civilian figures will not be mentioned here, but many went on to prosperous lives in the private sector. Several of the Ballard Family became county officials, and even John Goode held several county offices in Craig. Few Confederate officers ever achieved as high military commands again.

---

[16] Bostic and Reynolds, Bostic Cemetery list; Rose Family Group Sheets, compiled by Pat Nichols, Sinks Grove, WV.

[17] Hellems Diary, Aug. 17, 1889; Ibid., Jan. 4, 1893; Ibid., Dec. 7, 1894; Bostic Interview, Apr. 1988.

[18] Morton, Monroe, 323-325; Morton, Alleghany, 132.

Only in rare instances, such as in the case of Fitzhugh Lee, did some command forces in the Spanish-American War. One man of interest, John Echols, moved from Union following the war and settled in Staunton. He devoted the rest of his life to business and was a strong supporter of the Chesapeake and Ohio Railroad. Echols died in Staunton on May 24, 1896.[19]

And the "Union Hole"? Paint Bank went through a "golden period" following the war. The Farmer's Alliance found Paint Bank in 1890, and a hotel was built there. In World War I, there was strip mining in the area. The logging interests, in the guise of land companies, bought up much available land. When the logging interests moved to the Pacific Northwest, so did the "golden period." It never recovered, nor did it return. Now, in the 1990's, the trees have come back in force. Wild life still abounds down bumpy dirt and gravel roads. Potts' Creek looks more like a river, and Ewin's Run can even be imposing after a heavy rain. It is not hard to imagine those Civil War-era yeoman farmers. It may be harder to imagine those same yeoman farmers supporting the policies of Lincoln. Yet, for some, that is what happened. If this shatters a gold-gilt image on one people, one thought process, good. After all, the individual is, and was, unique.

---

[19] Morton, Monroe, 323-325; Ibid., 339; Ibid., 467-468; Question 39, John Goode testimony, Sept. 9, 1872, in John Goode SCC claim, National Archives; James L. Nichols, General Fitzhugh Lee--A Biography (Lynchburg, VA: H.E. Howard, Inc., 1989), 161; Ibid., 164-165.

108th Virginia Militia from Volume 20, Confederate Rosters, located in the Virginia State Library and Archives, Richmond

Co. A

Madison M. Ballentine	Capt.
Alexander K. Parker	1st Lt.
Andrew J. Wylie	2nd Lt.
James W. Parker	1st Sgt.
Robert A. Reaburn	2nd Sgt.
David R.P. Parker	3rd Sgt.
Henry J. Young	1st Corp.
James A. Dunsmore	2nd Corp.

Calvin H. Burdette
Robert A. Boyd
William L. Bostick
Henry A. Bostick
James L. Bostick
Robert F. Bostick
Adison Bostick
John B. Beamer
John A. Ballantine
Charles Campbell
John E. Campbell
John P. Campbell
Newton Dickson
James A. Dooley
Calvin Erskine
G.W. Erskine
Joel Garman
William H. Hogshead
Hiram McC. Hogshead
Washington McC. Hogshead
Charles A. Humphreys
James S. Hawkins
Christopher C. Hoke
Andrew Irons
John W. Johnson
Edmondson C. Kale
Michael Kelly
Thomas S. Murvill
James Marin
Richard D. McDowel

Charles A. Nickel
Robert A. Patton
Albert D. Patton
William H.H. Parker
Thomas B. Parker
Robert G. Parker
William Scott
David Tomlinson
William C. Tomlinson
Daniel A. Vance
Benjamin Vanstavern
George Williams
James G. Young
George G. Young
John C. Young

Co. B

William S. Ruddell	Capt.
Abner H. Neel	1st Lt.
Edmond P. Legg	2nd Lt.
Samuel R. Watt	1st Sgt.
Harrison Lowery	2nd Sgt.

Mathew A. Armstrong
John M. Abbott
William A. Baker
Morgan Brown
Thomas H. Bland
William P. Bowyer
James Blaker
Thomas Crosier
John H. Caldwell
Thomas E. Dickson
Nicholas A. Dunbar
Gasaway G. Eggleston
James Eggleston
Richard C. Eggleston
Augustus Eades
Andrew A. Fulkiner
Richard Faudrel
George Faudrel
Archibald Gregory
Lewis Griffith
Irvin B. Hull
James D. Hooker
James M. Haptonstore
James Lawhorn
Thomas Landers
Edmond P. Legg
Charles L. Lowry
Robert B. McCaleb
Jonathan M. McCormmach
Joseph P. McCormmack
James Miller
Allen H. Moses
Thomas J. Milller
George W. Mourn

Ephraim Neel
John K. Neel
Jacob A. Neel
Joseph O. Neel
James M. Neel
John Powel
Frank D. Robertson
William Sears
Austin Smith
Lewis F. Smith
William O. Smith
Fleming R. Traner
William Z. Wickline
Andrew L. Wickline
John E. Wickline
G.W. Wickline
Floyd Wickline
John D. Vance
Henry R. Vance
Henry W. Vance
Anderson C. Vass
James H. Vaughan

Co. C

Washington Lemons	Capt.
Joshua Leach	1st Lt.
Joshua H. Tracy	1st Sgt.
George A. Boyd	2nd Sgt.
Andrew O. Miller	2nd Sgt.
William A. Staton	Corp.
E. Fenton	Corp.
Trace L. Fox	Corp.--1/21/1862

William R. Armstrong		William F. Lemons	
William Archer		James R. Lynch	
Alexander Bowyer		Andrew Leach	1/21/1862
James P. Burdett		Edmund Leach	1/21/1862
Marion F. Bruffy		James A. Lemons	1/21/1862
Chapman K. Baker		Algernon S. Martin	
James H. Bostick		William F. Miller	
Andrew A. Burns		Josiah Minnick	
Cephalus Black		Joseph A. Miller	
Paterfield A. Boyd	1/21/1862	William Massy	1/21/1862
Michael A. Becket	1/21/1862	John Mann	
Archibald M. Carter	1/21/1862	James McAlister	
Andrew L. Dunsmore		John McCoy	1/21/1862
Charles L. Dunsmore		Samuel W. Nickell	
John Dunsmore, Sr.		Charles P. Nickell	
John W. Dunsmore		William Neel	
George W. Dunsmore		George Nickell	1/21/1862
William Donley		Robert Perry	
John M. Erskin		Newman Reynolds	1/21/1862
Archibald Erskin		Andrew J. Surber	
George W. Folden		Isacc J. Scott	
William Fenton		James H. Scott	
John W. Gray	1/21/1862	thomas N. Smith	
John Glover	1/21/1862	Harrison Scott	1/21/1862
William A. Hasten		George Scott	1/21/1862
William Hardburger	1/21/1862	Oliver Thompson	
John W. Hoke		John L. Vass	
John E. Jarvis		Austin A. Woodson	
William A. Jones		Rovert Wiley	
Albert G. Knapp		David S. Wickline	
Abner U.G. Leach		Jacob Wickline	
Jackson W. Lemons		Anderson M. Waitte	1/21/1862
Robert Lemons		William J. Zimmerman	1/21/1862

John McCoy
Andrew Massy
Reuben Massy   1/21/1862

Co. D

Charles K. Budd	Capt.
Patrick H. Hawkins	Lt.
James K. Ballantine	Lt.
Otho Crebbs	Lt.
Cornelius Leach	1st Sgt.
Nathaniel B. Long	1st Corp.

John K. Burdett
Henry Byrnside
James H. Burdett
Rasputin M. Carter
Joseph F. Cook
George Cox
Thomas M. Crozier
William A. Carter
John DeHart
William C. DeHart
Isaac DeHart
James DeHart
Nicholas A. Dunbar
George W. Davis
Madison Davis
M.A. DeHart
William A. Francis
Giles A. Fawekes
Lewis A. Holmes
Amos A. Hansburger
Peter B. Honaker
Andrew G. Huffman
William J. Higginbotham
Henry A. Higginbotham
Philip Holsaple
William Irons
George Kouns
James Kershner
Andrew Y. Leach
William H. Lynch
James M. Miller
Thomas A. Miller
John McCay
John Nicholas
John F. Nelson

Andrew Prentice
Nathaniel H. Roberts
Lewis H. Smith
Thomas A. Smith
Price M. Spade
Lewis Steel
Newman Smith
Charles Talbert
Jacob W. Vance
James M. Wilson
William Woolvine
Henry Walburn
Philip Woolwine
Edward White

111

Co. E.

Gibbons G. Figgatt   Capt.
John M. Crozier   1st Lt.

Washington Arnold
John Abbot
John L. Bradly
James G. Bradly
Selvester Bradly
Robert Bland
Harvey J. Bland
Christopher C. Burns
George W. Crozier
William H. Crozier
Thomas M. Crozier
James Crozier
William Crowder
Lorenzo V. Crowder
Philip B. Crozier
Benjamin C. Carlisle
James M. Dunbar
Robert S. Dunbar
Thomas M. Dunbar
William A. Daugherty
Andrew J. Daugherty
William J. Evans
William T. Figgatt
Thomas Fury
William J. Foster
Alexander H. Groves
Thomas M. Hepler
Leonard W. Hellems
Thomas M. Hellems
John Hipes
Abner A. Jarvis
James N. Linton
George A. Linton
Thomas Landers
James Myers
Samuel B. Modesherd
Archibald Miller
Robert McClowney
Richard Naga

William Patton
William Pritt
James Roach
James Row
Joseph Rumsey
Jackson Rose
William M. Smith
Thomas B. Steel (later prom. to 1st Sgt.)
Adam Smith
William Shaeves
Anderson Wiseman

112

Co. F

A.J. Sames	Capt.
Henderson Reid	1st Lt.
James A. Bostick	2nd Lt.
Edward Vass	1st Sgt.
Charles T. Hogshead	2nd Sgt.
John A. Daughterty	1st Corp.
Geisham H. Keys	2nd Corp.

Madison A. Burns
William S. Bostick
Edward P. Balard
John R. Booker
Joseph W. Carlisle
George W. Carnefix
Daniel Campbell
William Dodd
Martin Doyle
William Groves
Porris Goodall
Isaac M. Honaker
Jeremiah M. Holsapple
Samuel P. Holsapple
John W. Holsapple
Murtha Hickey
Francis M. Holylman
John F. Harper
Augustus Hickman
Henry Moss
Andrew J. Moss
John A. McMan
Adam Mentz
James W. Mentz
Thomas J. Miller
Brownlee H. Parker
James A. Parker
Joseph Read
Bernah Reed
James H. Reed
James Reed
John M. Reed
Charles Remley
John H. Ridgway

James F. Sanders
Daniel J. Stull
William C. Shaver
Benjamin F. Sames
Francis Scott
Christopher G. Shiers
William M. Smith
George W.J. Thomas
David Vanburen
John W. Vance
Hudson Vanstavern
William C. Vanstavern
Jacob A. Wickline
Michael Winbiener
Christopher Young

Co. G

Augustus B. McNeer	Capt.
Allan J. Piles	1st Lt.
William Smith	2nd Lt.
Alexander McClarin	1st Sgt.
Andrew J. Mahon	2nd Sgt.
John Murphy	3rd Sgt.
John W. Piles	4th Sgt.
William H. Fuller	1st Corp.
Charles W. Walker	2nd Corp.
Madison Pine	3rd Corp.
Chalres B. Mitchell	4th Corp.

William M. Archy
William L. Armontrout
Newton Allen
Washington Arnold
Andrew J. Abbott
John Ballard
Lewis C. Bowyer
Henry S. Ballard
John Bostick
Peter B. Bostick
Nelson J. Bostick
Thomas C. Bostick
William R. Boggess
Stewart Bare
Alexander Bradly
Cornelius Ballard
Henry C. Campbell
G.W. Carson
Augustus Campbell
William P. Campbell
Samuel M. Clark
Thomas M. Crozier
Philip Collins
Clemins J. Campbell
Charles Campbell
James M. Dunbar
Thomas M. Dunbar
William P. Deorieux
John J. Fisher   drummer
William P. Glover
Alexander Smith

John B. Honaker
Ephraim S. Honaker
John Hecht
Issac Honaker
Thomas Helms
Andrew J. Johnson
Charles B. Johnson
Richard L. Johnson
William O. Johnson
Michael Kady
Augustus Laughorn
Asberry H. Lynch
James N. Linton
Overton Long
Lewis J. Mann
Caperton McCarty
William R. McNeer
Alexander S. Martin
Abram Myers
Samuel B. Motesherd
William F. Nelson
James A. Pine
Judson Pool
George J. Piles
Elisha Rains
William Ryan
Floyd Rain
Jackson Rose
Joseph Ramsey
James Roach

John S. Smith
William M. Smith
Joel G. Shepherd
Thomas A. Teas
George Wickle
James Wickle
John J. Wallace

BIBLIOGRAPHY

Ames, Susie M., ed., County Court Records of Accomack--Northampton, Virginia 1640-1645. Vol. 10, Charlottesville: U. of Virginia Press, 1973, Virginia Historical Society Documents.

Armentrout, Lafe. Telephone Interview. Apr. 1992.

Bahlman, William F. "Down in the Ranks," Journal of the Greenbrier Historical Society. Vol. II, No. 2, Oct. 1970, 39-93.

Ballard, Margaret B. William Ballard--A Genealogical Record of his Descendants in Monroe County. Baltimore: Pridemark Press, c. 1957.

Boehm, Robert B. "The Unfortunate Averell," Civil War Times Illustrated. Volume V, No. 5, August 1966. Gettysburg: Historical Times Inc., 1966, 30-36.

Border Watchman. Union, WV. Obituaries.

Bostic, Jack and Layman Reynolds. Schematic Representation of the Jarvis Cemetery, Back Valley of Monroe County, West Virginia. New Castle, VA: unpublished, 1988.

Bostic, Orville H. Sr. Personal Interview. Apr. 1988.

----. Personal Interview. Aug. 1988.

----. Personal Interview, Oct. 1988.

----. Personal Interview. June 1989.

----. Personal Interview. Dec. 1989.

----. Personal Interview. Jan. 1990.

----. Personal Interview. Apr. 1990.

Bowman, John S., ed. The Civil War Day by Day. Greenwich, CT: Brompton Books, 1989.

Braake, Alex L. ter. "Postal History of the James River and Kanawha Turnpike," West Virginia History, published by Archives and History Division, State Museum, Vol XXXIII, No. 1, Oct. 1971, 27-54 (originally from American Philatelic Congress Book, Vol. 36, Oct. 1970, 31-52).

Bradley, James. Personal Interview. Jan. 1993.

Brown, Louis A. The Salisbury Prison--A Case Study of Confederate Military Prisons 1861-1865. Wendell, NC: Avera Press, 1980.

Burton, Charles T., comp. Botetourt County, Virginia, Early Settlers, n.p., n.d.

Cohen, Stan. The Civil War in West Virginia--A Pictorial History. Charleston: Pictorial Histories Publishing Company, 1976.

Comstock, Jim, ed. West Virginia Heritage Encyclopedia, Volume 1--Supplemental Series. Richwood, WV: author, 1974.

Confederate Veteran. N.A. Dunbar. Vol. XXXIII, No. 5. May, 1925. Reproduced Broadfoot's Bookmark, 187.

Cook, Dorothy. Telephone Interview. Jan. 1990.

Damewood, Mabel Lee. About Craig Valley. New Castle, VA: Craig Co. Historical Society, n.d.

Daughters of the American Revolution. Lineage Book of the National Society of the Daughters of the American Revolution, Volume 151. 1919, 2nd Set. Washington, D.C., 1936. [Early lineage books may not be fully accurate.]

Davis, William C. The Battle of New Market. Baton Rouge: Louisiana State U. Press, 1975.

Dorman, John Frederick. Westmoreland County, Virginia Order Books 1690-1698, Parts I, II, III. Washington, D.C.: n.p., 1962-1964.

----. ed. "Prince William County, Virginia Order Book 1759-1761," the Virginia Genealogist, Vol. 20, No. 1, Jan.-Mar., 1976, 35-44.

Evans, Norma Pontiff. Monroe County (West) Virginia Marriages: A Compiled List 1799-1850. Beaumont, TX: Tony Reyes Printing, 1985.

Fields, Frank. 28th Virginia Infantry. Lynchburg, VA: H.E. Howard Inc., 1985.

Fothergill, Augusta B. Wills of Westmoreland County, Virginia 1654-1800. n.p.: Appeals Press, 1925.

Gallia County Historical Society. Cemeteries of Springfield Township. Gallipolis, OH: Gallia Co. Historical Society, 1979.

Glenwood Cemetery, Washington, D.C.

Harris, William C. "Southern Unionist Critique of the Civil War," Civil War History, John T. Hubbell, ed., Vol. XXXI, No. 1, March 1985, 39-56.

Hellems, William M. Diary. Paint Bank, VA: n.p., n.d.

Howe, Thomas J. The Petersburg Campaign--Wasted Valor--June 15-18, 1864. Lynchburg, VA: H.E. Howard, Inc., 1988.

Hurst, Lucy Bryant. Paxton Family Group Sheets. Roanoke, VA.

Johnson, Patricia Givens. The United States Army Invades the New River Valley. Christiansburg, VA: Walpa Publishing, 1986.

Johnston, A.S. Captain Beirne Chapman and Chapman's Battery. Reprint from Monroe Historical Society. Union, WV: Monroe Watchman, 1991.

Johnston, Jane Echols and Brenda Williams. Hard Times, 1861-1865. Volume II. New Castle, VA: n.p., 1990.

LDS. Alleghany County Wills and Inventories No. 1, 1822-1837. filmed by Genealogical Society of Utah, 1953.

Linton, Ruby Bostic. Personal Interview. March 1990.

----. Personal Interview. Sept. 1991.

Lloyd, Hazel. "A Virginia Family." Jarvis Family Notes. Vol. I, No. 3. San Jose, CA: Rose Family Association, 1971, 70.

Lonn, Ella. Desertion During the Civil War. New York: The Century Co., 1928.

Lowry, Terry. September Blood--The Battle of Carnefex Ferry. Charleston, WV: Pictorial Histories Publishing Co., 1985.

----. 22nd Virginia Infantry. Lynchburg, VA: H.E. Howard Co., 1988.

Martin, Nora Bragg. Linton Family Group Sheets. Newport News, VA.

----. Persinger Family Group Sheets.

Martin, Viola. Personal Interview. March 1989.

----. Personal Interview. Nov. 1989.

McAllister, W.M. "Alleghany Roughs, or Carpenter's Battery,"
Confederate Veteran. Vol. XIII, No. 8, Aug. 1905.
Reproduced Broadfoot's Bookmark, 365-366.

McKinney, Tim. The Civil War in Fayette County West Virginia.
Charleston, WV: Pictorial Histories Publishing Co., 1988.

----. Robert E. Lee at Sewell Mountain: The West Virginia
Campaign. Charleston, WV: Pictorial Histories Publishing
Co., Inc., 1990.

McManus, Howard Rollins. The Battle of Cloyds Mountain--The
Virginia and Tennessee Railroad Raid--April 19-May 19,
1864. Lynchburg, VA: H.E. Howard, Inc., 1989.

McPherson, James M. Ordeal by Fire--The Civil War and
Reconstruction. New York: Alfred A. Knopf, 1982.

Monroe County Court House. Loose Papers--Civil War File.

Monroe Watchman. Union, WV. Obituaries.

Morton, Oren. A Centennial History of Alleghany County,
Virginia. Harrisonburg, VA: C.J. Carrier Company, 1986.

----. History of Monroe County, West Virginia. Baltimore, MD,
Regional Publishing Company, 1980.

Newlin, William Henry. An Account of the Escape of Six Federal
Soldiers from Prison at Danville, Virginia. Cincinnati:
Methodist Book Concern, 1870.

Nichols, James L. General Fitzhugh Lee--A Biography.
Lynchburg, VA: H.E. Howard, Inc., 1989.

Nichols, Pat. Comp. Rose Family Group Sheets. Sinks Grove,
WV.

Nicklin, John Bailey Calvert. "Descendants of Captain Robert
Behethland of Jamestown," Part 2. William and Mary
Quarterly. Series 2, Vol. 9, No. 3, July 1929, 175-185.

Nofi, Albert A. Opening Guns--Fort Sumter to Bull Run, 1861.
Series--Eyewitness to the Civil War, Vol. I. New York:
Combined Books, 1988.

Official Records of the Union and Confederate Armies.
Washington, DC: Government Printing Office, 128 Vols.

Ohio Roster Commission. Official Roster of the Soldiers of the
State of Ohio in the War of the Rebellion, Vol. X.
Cincinnati: Ohio Roster Commission, 1889.

Perkins, Louise Collins. "Some Residents Supported the North."
Virginia Review/Highlander. 6 June 1989.

----. Wolf Family Group Sheets.

Phillips, David L., ed. War Stories: Civil War in West Virginia.
Leesburg, VA: Gauley Mount Press, 1991.

Reynolds, Layman. Personal Interview. Sept. 1991.

Reynolds, Thurman. Personal Interview. July 1990.

Scott, J.L. Lowry's, Bryan's, and Chapman's Batteries.
Lynchburg, VA: H.E. Howard, 1986.

Sparacio, Ruth and Sam, comps. Virginia County Court Records--
Stafford County, Virginia--Will Book (liber o) 12 July 1748-
July Court 1767. McLean, VA: compilers, n.d.

State of West Virginia. Land Department, State Auditor's Office.
Sim's Index to Land Grants in West Virginia. Charleston,
WV: Rose City Press, 1952.

Tatum, Georgia. Disloyalty in the Confederacy. Chapel Hill,
NC: U. of North Carolina Press, 1934.

Torrence, Clayton, comp. Virginia Wills and Administrations
1632-1800. Richmond: William Byrd Press, 1930.

Turk, David Scott. "Mysterious Death of a Southern Unionist."
Rose Family Bulletin. Vol. XXIV, No. 95, September 1989.
San Hose, CA: Rose Family Association, 1989, 3433-3437.

United States National Archives. Census materials. RG29. 1820,
1830, 1850, 1860, Monroe County; 1860 Craig County.

----. Compiled Service Records of Soldiers who fought from
Volunteer Organizations in Virginia. RG109, M324, 108th
VA Militia, Chapman's Battery, 23rd Virginia Infantry, 60th
Virginia Infantry.

----. Compiled Service Records of Soldiers who fought from
Volunteer Union Soldiers who served in Organizations from
West Virginia. RG94, M508.

----. Confederate Business firms. RG109, M346, Confederate
Business Firms.

----. Letters Received by the Confederate Adjutant and Inspector
General. RG109, M474.

----. Letters Received by the Confederate Secretary of War.
RG109, M437.

----. Miscellaneous Rolls of Federal Prisoners 1861-65. RG249. Box 8, Roll no. 691.

----. Pension Record, George W. Glenn. RG15. No. 732,124, Soldier's Pension.

----. Pension Record, Gilbert Glenn. RG15.

----. Pension Record, Field A. Jarvis. RG15. No. 186,920, Appl. No. 240,545, Father's Pension for Morgan Taylor Jarvis.

----. Pension Record, John E. Jarvis. RG15. No. 695,530, Appl. No. 895,132, Soldier's Pension.

----. Pension Record, Sarah Wiley. RG15. No. 238,394, Cert. No. 186,977, Mother's Pension for Allen Benton Wiley.

----. Post Office Department. Reports of Site Locations. RG28, M1126, Roll 607.

----. Revolutionary War Pension and Bounty--Land Warrant Application Files--Field Jarvis. RG15. M804, Roll 1408.

----. Southern Claims Commission files, Records of the GAO, Records of the Third Auditor's Office, 1871-1880. RG217. Allen Campbell (Box 409), Susannah Abbott (Box 343), Charles L. Humphries, Adm. of Jesse Humphries (Box 339). Entry 732.

----. Southern Claims Commission Files, Records of the House. RG123. William Paxton and John Goode.

Virginia State Library and Archives. Alleghany County Wills and Inventories, No. 1.

----. Botetourt County Deeds.

----. Confederate Pension Applications, Act of 1902. Manerva Reynolds, John B. Linton, Henry Tingler. Richmond: Genealogical Society of Salt Lake City, Utah, 1990.

----. Confederate Rosters, bound copy. Volume 20.

----. Craig County Order Book 2, 1860-63.

----. Westmoreland County Deeds, Reel 14.

----. Westmoreland County Order Books, 1705-1721.

----. Westmorleand Inventories and Settlements of Estates, No. 4.

----. WV Vital Statistics.

Wallace, Jr., Lee A. A Guide to Virginia Military Organizations 1861-1865. Lynchburg, VA: H.E. Howard, Inc., 1986.

Wesley, Charles H. Collapse of the Confederacy. Washington, DC: The Associated Publishers, Inc., 1937.

West Virginia University. Roy Bird Cook collection. Acquired, 1961.

Whitten, Joida, ed. Abstracts of Bedford County, Virginia Wills, Inventories and Accounts. Dallas, TX: Taylor Publishing Co., 1968.

Works Progress Administration. Monroe County, West Virginia, Vol. 3, Wills and Inventory. Washington, DC: n.p., 1936.

Index

Abbott, John, 82; Susannah, 81-82
Adams, Henderson, 50
Anthony, William, 12
Armentrout, Abraham, 16, 32,
    105; Allen, 5, 32, 34, 81, 105
    Bethsaida, 105; family, 12;
    Lafayette, 105; Michael
    Arritt, 17
Arnett, William, 67
Atkins, John, 33; Robert, 33
Averell, William W. 50, 58-68,
    79-81
Bagge, Mary, xv
Baker, William 25
Ballard, Baldwin, 24, 28; Beverly,
    52, 79; family, 12, 105;
    Jeremiah, 23; Lewis, 23, 45,
    71; William, 42-43, 55-56;
    William G. 68
Battle of Cedar Creek, 92
Battle of Chancellorsville, 47
Battle of Chickamauga Creek, 47,
    77
Battle of Cloyd's Mountain, 78
Battle of Cold Harbor, 84
Battle of Droop Mountain, 47, 60-
    61, 69
Battle of Dry Creek, 60
Battle of First Manassas, 2, 3, 4,
    18, 36
Battle of Fort Stevens, 86
Battle of Gauley Bridge, 4
Battle of Gettysburg, 47, 57, 77
Battle of Kelly's Ford, 50
Battle of Kernstown, 86
Battle of Lewisburg, 38-39, 78
Battle of Lynchburg, 84, 92
Battle of New Market, 82
Battle of Philippi, 3, 4, 18
Battle of Romney, 4
Battle of Spotsylvania Courthouse,
    84

Battle of the Monocacy, 85
Battle of the Wilderness, 84
Battle of Waynesboro, 94
Battle of White Sulphur Springs,
    47, 59, 75
Baxter, Sidney S., 32
Beane, family 25
Beckley, Albert, 5
Been, Thomas N., 51
Beirne, Andrew, 21; Oliver, 39-41,
    79
Berden, Harrison, 64
Bickman,---, 79
Blair, Montgomery, 85
Boggs, Fielding, 33
Bostic, Alexander, 91; Emma, 105;
    family, 6, 25; James, 6, 18,
    19, 25, 59, 91, 98, 101, 102;
    Jane Jarvis, 6, 58-59, 61, 91,
    101-102; Jesse, 6; Lelia, 101;
    Marion Columbus, 58, 91,
    98, 101; Wilbur C. 101-102
Bourn, James, xiv
Bragg, Adam, 32; Braxton, 76;
    David, 33
Breckinridge, John C., 78-79, 84
Brice, Edmon, 64
Brown, John, 27
Buchanan, James, 78
Butler family, xv
Bryan's Battery, 13
Byers, Peter, 59
Byrnside, James, 21
Cale, John S., 25
Camp, Robert, 18
Campbell, Allen, 81; Archibald,
    18; Lysander, 59, 70;
    Matthew, 52
Caperton, Allen Taylor, 3, 11, 14,
    40-44, 93, 98, 105; family, 9
Carpenter, family, 9
Carper, family, 53
Castle Thunder, 32, 45, 64, 78
Chapman, Augustus Alexandria, 3-
    5, 8, 11, 13, 14, 17, 20, 23,

28, 32, 34-35, 39-40, 55-56, 59, 70, 75; family, 9; George Beirne, 35, 91
Chapman's Battery, 4, 59
Childs, Robert, 74
Clark, William C., 54; William F. 59
Clarke, John, 30
Collins, Merit, 29-30
Committee of Safety. Alleghany County, 22, 59
Comer, John, 18
Confiscative Act, 55
Connaway, George E. 96-97
Conscription Act, 35-37, 70
Cox, Jacob, 3, 6, 18, 24, 38, 50
Craig's Creek, 52, 64, 65, 72
Crook, George, 33, 38, 78-79, 81, 83, 85-86
Crow's Tavern, 74
Damron, William, 59
Danville Prison, 71
Davis, Jefferson, 40
Deneaux, William P., 21
Drake, Mary, 101
Dropping Lick, 52
Duffie, Alfred, 61
Dunbar, Nancy, 13; Nicholas Augustus, 13, 92
Dunn, Herbert, 59
Early, Jubal, 85, 91
Eastern District Station, 45
Echols, John, 11-13, 14, 44, 56-57, 60, 65, 66, 68, 74-76, 88, 106
Eggleston, --, 25
Ellison, fmaily, 51; Pauline, 70
Emancipation Proclamation, 52
England, xiii, xv
Erskine, William, 15, 51
Ervine, Joseph, 13
Field, Abraham (II), xv; Abram, xv; Elizabeth, xv; Frances, xv
Figgatt, Gibbons, 13, 21, 24, 32; Jane, 13; Thomas A. 13

Finney, William W., 17
Floyd, John Buchanan, 5, 7, 19, 20, 23, 27
Fort Sumter, 14
Foxhall, John, xiv
Fridley, family, 66; Richard, 93; William N., 93
Gaines Mill, 89
Garten, Goodall, 29
Glenn, family, 8; Frank, 96
Goode, family, 53; John, 1, 12, 52-53, 65, 105; William, 53, 65
Grant, Ulysses S., 78, 84-85
Great Kanawha River, 18
Greenbrier River, 74
Griffith, Thomas G., 94
Hamilton, Robert, 18
Hancock, Edward, 65
Harper's Ferry Raid, 27
Hastings, William, 21
Hayes, Rutherford B., 37
Hellems, John L., 37; Leonard, 80, 82; Mason V., 25, 69; William M. 100
Hepler, David (Sr.), 74
Heroes of America, 88
Heth, Henry, 17, 38-40, 44, 56-57
Hogshead, James, 81
Hook, Madison, 66, 67
Houston, S.R., 11, 30, 38, 41-42, 46, 58, 59-60, 65-66, 79, 98, 99
Huffman, James, 72
Hull, Irvine B., 21; J.A.I., 21
Humphreys, A.I., 21
Humphries, Charles K. 93; family, 64; Harvey, 93; Jesse, 66, 93, 104; Smith, 13, 14
Hunter, David, 84, 85
Hutchinson, George W., 21
Indian Creek, 79, 103
Indiana. 11th Infantry, 3
Irvin, Joseph, 59
Island Ford Bridge, 67

Jackson, Thomas J. ("Stonewall"), 18, 41, 57; William L. ("Mudwall") 48-49, 65, 67, 79-80
Jackson River, 16
Jackson River Depot, 78
James River and Kanawha Turnpike, 15, 65, 73, 85
Jamison, George M., 93
Jarvis, Catherine, xv; Eleanor, xv; Elizabeth, xvi; family, xiii, 2, 6, 8, 10, 59, 86, 95, 100; Field, xvi; Field A., 2, 12-13, 22, 32, 36-37, 71, 82, 83, 90, 96, 100-101; James,xv; Jane, xv, 6, 13-14; Jane Richardson, 25; John, xiv, xv, xvi, 90; John (II), vi, xvi; John (III), xvi; John E., 5-7, 32, 86, 94-97, 101; Joseph, xix, 2, 37, 101; Margery, xvi; Matilda, 37, 101; Morgan T., 86, 90, 95, 97; Nancy Dunbar, 13; Richard, xiii, xiv; Sallie, 96, 100; Sarah, xvi; Susannah, 16; Thomas, xvi; "Tillie", xix, 2, 101; Washington, xix, 32, 82, 83; "Winnie", 2, 101
Jenkins, Albert Gallatin, 78
Johnston, Joseph E., 35-36
Jones, Samuel, 51, 55, 65, 67, 74, 76
Jones-Imboden Raid, 48
Kanawha Valley Campaign, 27
Kelly, Henry J., 23
Kincaid, Mansen, 33
King, family, 66; George P., 93
Landcraft,---, 30
Lee, Fitzhugh, 65, 106; Robert E., 7, 18, 22, 36, 47, 57, 85, 89
Lemons, Washington, 28, 34
Leory, Henry, 87, 88, 92
Lewis, family, 16
Lightburn, Andrew Jackson, 44

Lincoln, Abraham, 3-4, 11, 14, 52, 92, 98-99, 106
Linton, Euphemia N., 37, 102; George A., 16, 36-37, 82, 83, 95, 102; James N., 16, 36, 86, 102; John Barton, 16, 92, 102; Mary S.E., 37; Sena, 86, 102; Susan, 102; Susannah, 86; William, 102
Lively, Wilson, 51, 56
Longstreet, James, 71, 77
Looney, Alexander C., 51; Moses, 51
Loring, William Wing, 27, 41, 43-44, 56
Loyal League, 82-83
Loyal Order of the Heroes of America, 49, 50, 83, 87
Mann, Jefferson I., 33
Marcum, James, 90
Martin, Benjamin, 95-96; Nicholas, 45
McAllister, Robert, 8; Thompson, 9, 59, 99, 105
McClellan, George, 3, 35, 36
McDaniel, M., 91
Middle Mountain, 62-63
Miskill, Patrick, xiv
Morgan, John J., 36, 52
Mountain View Church, 53
Myers, Adam, 51
Neel, Allen G., 21, 103-104; Frank, 27, 100, 103-104
Noble, David, 28-29, 68; Joseph, 29
North Carolina. Salisbury, 44-45, 71
Ohio. Gallia County, 8, 46, 81, 86, 90, 104; Pike County, 101; Portsmouth, 95; troops, 3
Ohio Infantry. 47th, 53; 173rd, 90; 36th, 79, 194th, 95
Ohio River, 44, 46
Ould, Robert, 45

Parker, family, 6, 25; James, 18
Patton, John, 18; George, 8, 13,
    20, 58, 91; Napoleon, 25;
    William Tristam, 4
Paxton, "Lyda", 89; Joseph
    Abraham Lincoln, 90;
    William, 62-64, 72-74, 85,
    87, 103
Pennsylvania. Adams County, 9
Persinger, Aaron, 104; Nancy, 93;
    Nash, 93, 95; Seth Linton,
    95; William, 93; Zeb, 93, 104
Peter's Mountain, 52
Peyton, Charles S., 92-93
Philips, Delor, 64
Pickett's Charge, 57
Pool, John, 49
Potts' Creek, 12, 16, 24, 36, 106
Potts' Mountain, 37, 80
Potterfield, George, 3
Price, Samuel, 75
Pritt, William, 92
Quickel, William, 93
Railroad. Baltimore & Ohio, 3;
    Virginia and Tennessee, 15,
    60-61, 78
Randolph, George Wythe, 39-40
Rappahannock River, 48
Reed, Henderson, 19, 104
Reynolds, Andrew Cambel, 89-90,
    103; Elizabeth Jane, 87;
    James, 52, 57; John Landon,
    57; Mary Jane Goode, 89
Rich Patch Valley, 66, 76, 93
River. Great Kanawha, 18;
    Greenbrier, 74; Jackson, 16;
    Ohio, 44, 46
Rose, family 10; Harvey, 31, 105;
    Jackson, 5, 7, 20-21, 24, 30-
    32, 45-46, 89, 90; James, 69;
    Manerva Ann, 89, 103, 104-
    105; Ruth Wolf, 31, 67, 104;
    Tabitha, 31
Rosecrans, William S., 7, 20, 50

Rowan, Allen Caperton, 13;
    Frances, 25; John M. 5-6, 13,
    19, 23, 34
Rozier, David (Jr), xv
Rutledge, William E. 70, 82, 83,
    102
Ryder,---, 25
Saffore, Benjamin D. 64
Salem Raid, 47, 62, 76, 79
Salt Sulphur Mountain Lake
    Turnpike, 15
Saunders,---, 55
Scammon, Elichim, 50
Second Creek, 81
Seddon, James A., 55, 56, 75, 88
Sequestration Act, 55
Sexton, thomas, 28-30, 33
Shanklin, Davidson, 18
Sheppard,---, 94
Sheridan, Philip, 91
Sherman, William Tecumseh, 92,
    94
Sherwood,---, 38
Shirkey, Charlton, 59
Siege of Petersburg, 86, 89, 92,
    94, 97
Siege of Vicksburg, 53, 77, 92
Sigel, Franz, 78, 84
Sinking Creek, 61
Smith, Elizabeth J., 70; family, 51;
    H. DeWitt, 70; John C. 93;
    Kirby, 97; William, 5, 24,
    34; Major, 33
Spessard, family, 53
Starks, John, 80-81
Staton, Bartholomew, xvi;
    Margery, xvi
Steadman,---, 90
Stuart, James Ewell Brown
    ("JEB"), 50
Stull, family, 66
Swamp Guards, 33
Sweet Springs and Kanawha
    Turnpike, 61

Sweet Springs Mountain, 42, 65, 79
Teas, Thomas, 21
Tennessee. Nashville, 90
Third Battle of Winchester, 91
Tiffany, Hugh, 2, 4, 18
Tingler, Henry, 12, 39, 82, 83, 102
Trainer, Fleming, 90-91
Trenor, Fleming, 69
Tucker, John, 33
Turnpike. James River and Kanawha, 15, 65, 73, 84; Salt Sulphur and Mountain Lake, 15; Sweet Springs and Kanawha, 61
U.S. Troops. 8th Regiment, Virginia Volunteers, 29; 8th Virginia, 29
Van Buren, Martin, 74
Vaulx, James, xv
Vickers, Edward, xvi; Elizabeth, xvi
Virginia. Abbott, 12; Accomack County, xiii; Alleghany County, 2, 4, 8-9, 12-13, 17, 22, 25, 27, 30, 35, 38, 54, 58, 59, 66, 71, 74, 78, 86, 87, 88, 89; Amherst County, xvi; Botetourt County, 63, 87; Callaghans, 58, 67; Christiansburg, 83, 87; Covington, 12, 14, 58, 65-67; Craig County, 1, 2, 4, 8, 12, 15-17, 22, 25, 27, 32, 35, 36, 49, 52, 57, 61, 71, 78, 81, 84, 86, 87, 104, 105; Craig Court House, 12, 14, 22, 65; Danville, 71; Dublin, 15; Eastern Shore, xiii; Fincastle, 63, 73; Gaines Mills, 89; Giles County, 17, 61, 91; Highland County, 61; Jackson River, 16; Lexington, 84, 89; Manassas, 36; Montgomery County, 87; New Castle, 12, 84; Northampton County, xii; Paint Bank, 12, 13, 16, 20-21, 25, 32, 53, 58, 69, 71, 79, 100, 102, 103, 105; Prince William County, xiv; Pulaski County, 15; Richmond, 28, 32, 36, 42, 44, 49, 59; Rockbridge County, xvi; Salem, 62, 64, 66; Stafford, xiv; Staunton, 65; Tidewater, xii; Westmoreland County, xiii, xiv, xv, xvi, xvii; Winchester, 91; Yorktown, 36
Virginia (West Virginia). Back Valley, 34, 51, 69, 82, 83; Barbour County, 3; Carnifex Ferry, 5, 20; Charleston, 18, 27, 44, 90; Charlestown, 95, 105; Cotton Hill, 6-7, 23; Fayette County, 6, 20; Forest Run, 6, 19, 25; Gap Mills, 13, 21; Gauley Bridge, 3, 5-6, 18, 74; Greenbrier County, 7, 17, 27, 33, 49; Greenbrier Valley, 60, 61; Greenville, 12, 23, 52, 70; Hardy County, 33; Harper's Ferry, 27, 97; Jefferson County, 95; Kanawha County, 29-30; Kanawha Valley, 5, 19, 43, 46; Lewisburg, 35, 38, 58, 61; Meadow Bluff, 7; Mercer County, 17, 37, 55; Monroe County, xiii, 1-2, 4-5, 8, 11, 14, 17-18, 21-23, 25, 27, 28, 30, 31, 35, 38, 40, 45, 49, 50, 55, 68, 70, 71, 75, 78, 79, 86, 87, 91; New River, 30; Pack's Ferry, 28; Pocohontas County, 25, 49, 60; Point Pleasant, 44; Potts' Creek, xvii, 12, 16, 25, 36, 100, 106; Potts' Creek

Valley, 31; Putnam County, 95; Raleigh, 55; Red Sulphur Springs, 30; Rock Camp, 42; Rocky Point, 21; Romney, 3; Salt Sulphur Springs, 39, 50, 52; Sewell Mountain, 7; Sweet Springs, 16, 41, 58, 61, 85; Sweet Springs Mountain, 42, 66, 79; Sweet Springs Valley, 19; Union, 12, 17, 35, 52, 81; Waiteville, 12; White Sulphur, 29; White Sulphur Springs, 37, 58, 59; Willow Bend, 79

Virginia and Tennessee Railroad, 15, 60, 61, 62, 78

Virginia Convention, 14

Virginia Infantry. 22nd, 8, 13, 20, 35, 37, 51, 58, 69, 87; 23rd, 59; 27th, 4, 18; 28th, 65, 89; 54th, 87; 60th, 91, 92

Virginia Militia. 19th Brigade, 4, 7, 17, 20, 23; 79th, 17; 86th 17; 108th, 4-6, 13, 18-19, 21, 24, 25, 28; 128th, 17; 151st, 17; 166th, 17; 189th, 8, 17; town of Union 2nd Class, 17

Wagamaster, Artmanus, xiv

Wallace, Lew, 3, 85

Washington family, xv

Webb, John, 15, 52

Widow Scott's Tavern, 62, 73, 74, 76, 85

Wiles, Henry, 33

Wiley, Allen B., 53-54, 104; James, 53; Sarah, 53, 104

William,---, 83

Williams, John S., 50-51

Wilson, Andrew, 83

Winder, John Henry, 32

Wingfield, Wyley, 18

Wise, Henry Alexander, 5, 7, 20, 27

Wolf, family, 66; Isaac R. 51, 93

Wylie, Dr. ---, 66-68

Wordon, John, xvi

Zimmerman, David, 84-85